W9-BSN-072

BOOKS BY JOHN RANDOLPH PRICE

The Superbeings

The Planetary Commission

Practical Spirituality

With Wings As Eagles

The Abundance Book

A Spiritual Philosophy for the New World

Empowerment: There is nothing that you cannot do, be, or have

A SPIRITUAL PHILOSOPHY FOR THE NEW WORLD

by John Randolph Price

Library of Congress Catalog Card Number 90-61586
International Standard Book Number 0-942082-11-7

Published by QUARTUS BOOKS
The Quartus Foundation for Spiritual Research, Inc.
P. O. Box 1768
Boerne, Texas 78006-6768

Printed in the United States of America

Cover art designed and produced by K. Eron Howell

This book is lovingly dedicated to the members of the international Quartus Society, and especially to those who participated in the 60-day non-human program and graduated with a lifetime commitment to Fourth Dimensional Living. You tested your wings in experimental flight and found the strength and power to soar beyond "this world" into the Realm of Cause. You are the Pathfinders ... and "greater works" will you do.

TABLE OF CONTENTS

INTRODUCTION

In 1988, hundreds of men and women around the world volunteered for an experiment in consciousness. For sixty days they were asked to live in another Dimension. Their assignment was to work in the laboratory of mind to achieve a new attitude of harmlessness and a deeper understanding of cause and effect, and then to move into the energies and vibrations of the Fourth Dimension— not as human beings but as Spiritual Beings of Light. After a period of assimilation they were to return in consciousness to "this world" and perform their mighty works of creative expression in the third dimensional plane of materiality.

What began as a sixty day experiment became a lifetime commitment, for the new understanding unequivocally documented the Ancient Truth that consciousness is cause and everything in the physical world is an effect of consciousness—individual and collective. The participants in this "Non-Human Program"—which is the theme of this book—began to realize, perhaps as never before, that it is impossible to heal a third-dimensional effect with a third-dimensional consciousness. Temporary relief may be evidenced, but in time the fake

9

plaster will fall and the old wall of scarcity, devastation, fear and futility will again be visible. The key, therefore, is to be *in* this world but not of it—and to be "not *of* it" means to rise into that already-fully-present state of consciousness called Divine Individualism and from there to extend the Light of Reality into the world of shadows. This is what I am asking of all who have caught the vision and who are speaking the word for peace to come forth in every mind, for love to flow forth from every heart, for forgiveness to reign in every soul, and for understanding to be the common bond.

The Winds of Change. Throughout the world today men and women are experiencing a shifting of values and the breaking up of the old forms, and they are stirred to action in a great array of causes. The vision of freedom and peace has inspired millions to throw off their shackles in a new spirit of independence. And the continuing storm of overpopulation, pollution, land erosion, deforestation and shrinking water levels has united people in a powerful new wave of activism to combat projected natural disasters, food scarcities, famine, and economic depression.

This activity ties right in with the global undertaking that began on December 31, 1986 to heal and harmonize Planet Earth and all forms of life hereon. But human consciousness alone will not turn the tide. We must not forget that Jesus prefaced the Great Commission to his disciples by directing them "*to the mountain.*" Before they were given the assignment to go into all the world to teach, save every creature, and heal all they touched, they were taken to a higher state of consciousness as symbolized by the mountain. And we must follow this example if we are to heal the world and save the planet.

Ageless Wisdom tells us that the most effective force in the world of individual beings is divine indifference and the ability to work from a center of peace to powerfully carry out the work. This "indifference" is simply being detached from mental misperceptions and binding emotional attractions which drain a person's energy and make him or her powerless as a world server. It is also said that when any activity of life is removed from the realm of spirituality, another sense of separation is created and exclusiveness "rules the impulse and reverses the good."

The solution to individual and planetary problems is obvious. We achieve a neutral attitude regarding the miscreations of the lower nature and refuse to be identified with anything except the Divine Consciousness of the Master Self. We commit to the *spiritual life* and recognize that every global activity and cause must come under the umbrella of spirituality. This would include the environment, education, economics, international relations, government and politics, social activism, science, and religion and philosophy—all being subsidiaries to the Parent Force of Love, Goodwill, and the World of Energies. We move "to the mountain" in consciousness, break the connection with our "human" sense of being, and become empowered—to the highest degree of which we are capable—with the Sacred Fire of our Divinity. Then we descend once again into "this world" to do our work with inspiration, illumination, intuition, inclusiveness, harmlessness, emotional control, and a highly developed quality of unconditional love—the spiritual attributes that will remove the seemingly unsolvable problems from our little worlds and the race as a whole.

Breaking the Ego Connection. You begin the journey to the mountain by going through a series of detachments, freeing yourself from the ego so that you may become infused with the Mind of the Master Self within. And you continue the process of detachment until you have surrendered every mental, emotional and physical pull. You release everything that has bound you to the wheel of struggle and strife; you willingly sacrifice the lesser to realize the Greater and you hold nothing back.

When you stop identifying yourself with the world of form (remember, you are in this world but not of it), and when you break the mental and emotional bondage to outer effects and illusion, you are removing the layers of

11

personality patterns that have surrounded your Divine Nature. And when the Real Being breaks through, your life is changed so dramatically that you begin to live in Heaven on Earth. The Fourth Dimension has been brought into the third. The problems, challenges, trials and tribulations experienced by the lower nature are no longer there because you are no longer living out of the lower nature. All desires, wants and needs have been taken over by the Master Self and are brought into manifestation according to the Higher Vision—which always means more than you conceived of before. In essence, you die to lack, limitation, unfulfillment, futility, conflict, despair, fear, guilt, sorrow and weakness and are reborn into the resurrected life of dominion and mastery.

The Vertical Message. The manuscript of this book was submitted to several major publishing houses in New York, and each one responded with the comment that the material was too vertical or specialized for a mass audience. I agree. It was not written for the masses, yet I believe with all my heart that the religion of the coming civilization will be a spiritual philosophy based on Individual Divinity. The average man and woman will one day find that the only church is within, that the only minister-teacher is the indwelling Spirit, and that the only power on Earth is Consciousness. In the meantime, there are those who have consented to *vertical* living, which means rising above ground level, and who are *specializing* in a particular line of endeavor called mastery. And it is these new vertical Wayshowers with their specialized dedication who are even now moving into the staging area to prepare us all for the Power and Glory of the Fifth Kingdom and the culmination of the Lord's Prayer.

To be a part of this advanced Force does not mean that you have to leave your body or renounce all the forms and experiences of this world. The purpose of the Non-Human Program is not to break the connection between the ideas of energy and form, nor to see the physical world as non-spiritual. Quite the opposite. The main thrust of the program is to balance the absolute with the relative and see the unity of spirit and matter—to know that in the energy of life and the manifestation of form, there is only oneness. But this unity cannot be seen through the aura of human consciousness. It can only be seen through the single eye of Divine Consciousness, and once seen, your individual world is totally transformed.

I have attempted to write this book with great clarity and to reach you with an easy flow of words. My intention is to help you give up everything that binds you to the world of effects, to sever the emotional attractions that are causing bondage in your life, and to sharpen your intuitive focus so that you can see through the illusion to reality. In the process you will find dynamic changes taking place in your life—including your health, finances, relationships, and creative expression. And when you move back into the mundane world you will be ready to assume your role and fulfill your purpose *as a spiritual being in physical form.*

Your spiritual family—men, women and children all over the world with an awakening consciousness—are waiting for you. They have come forth from every nation, from all races, from all religions, and they acknowledge no Master except the One within Whom they serve. You will recognize them immediately, and they will know you, and together you will go forth with great inspiration to transform this planet into the Heavenly Body that it was created to be—the beloved Earth, the Planet of Serenity—the home of the Forces of Light.

CHAPTER 1

The Non-Human Experience

There is a massive, humanly-created, highly charged band of negative energy within the race mind that is continually projecting itself into the consciousness of individual men and women. This is the "evil" that the religionists speak of and even those on the spiritual path are susceptible to it.

For example, in spite of all the metaphysical success stories many seekers of Truth continue to be lost in the darkness of loneliness, unfulfillment, insufficiency, illness, and conflict. There are men and women who meditate daily, go to church every Sunday, attend spiritual retreats, and read every new metaphysical book—yet their lives remain confused and chaotic. Of course, each case is different and all is a state of consciousness, but you would think that more people who are dedicated and committed to the spiritual way of life would one day find themselves free of the Big Ride—that old roller coaster with its combination of top-of-the-world and stomach-in-the-throat experiences.

Why can't we all be free? Because we continue to be connected through the ego to that malevolent force in collective consciousness which lowers our vibratory rate, thus attracting misery and misfortune into our lives. But there is a dark secret about this pernicious creation. *It has no real power!* Its only power is drawn from our individual energy fields, which means that it functions as a *vampire*— and its life is sustained only by the power that we give it. Therefore, the only reality it has is the state of being that it assumes when plugged into our vital essence—and the more we fight it, the more substantial it becomes in our experience.

Without treating a serious subject too lightly or insulting the famous Count from Transylvania by addressing this deviant energy of the collective mind as Dracula, let's bring this miscreation into physical form with a focus of our imagination and communicate directly with him. We might say...

''You have been preying on the energy of humankind since the descent into materiality, feeding upon our negative thoughts and emotions, gorging yourself and infesting us with living death. The time has come to be rid of you, for it is your parasitic energy that has infected the people of this world with sickness, poverty, war, destruction and death.

''We know that we created you. We acknowledge that we literally prayed you in with our fears, our greed, our intolerance, our bigotry, our hate, and our ignorance. But we have finally come to our senses and now it's time to pull the plug. We want to drive you back into your coffin and seal the lid permanently, cutting you off forever from the energy of our planetary family.''

In our imagination we see him standing in the shadows wearing his black cape—and we hear him say, ''Well my goodness—and that's a paradoxical statement for me— you certainly are audacious. Just who do you think you are, God? Personally, I believe that there will always be sufficiently mind-blind, emotionally-bent, ignorant, hateful, bigoted, and greedy people around to draw on— *oh what a lovely expression*—so I truly have nothing to fear. Do you really think that there is sufficient inherent goodness in the human heart to limit my insatiable appetite? Can you conceive for even one moment the religious zealots of every faith laying down their arms and agreeing to religious tolerance? Will you ever see the day when money is not worshipped by the majority of people on Earth? Can you imagine any political or economic system not being oppressive or exploitative in some way to some people? Will there ever be a time when war is not beautiful to a part of the world's population? Can the stain of man's harmfulness ever be removed from nature? Come on now, grow up!

"You unleashed me millions of years ago, and while your organized efforts may have denied me a few meals and caused an annoying weakness in my system, you certainly haven't incapacitated me. Oh, well, nearly two thousand years ago I did have a scare, but fortunately for me most of what that Man said and did was misinterpreted. And even though He released His energy to be a force for the new world, few have attained His Consciousness. So whom shall I fear? You people are a joke and I welcome your puny human attempts to thwart me. You see, that's what I am—*human*—and to attack me is to attack yourself. So give it your best shot and reap the consequences. This is going to be fun.''

Whether he knew it or not, our ''Dracula'' gave us the secret of removing him from our lives. He challenged our humanhood, but we will not respond with human energy for that would only provide him with more delicious appetizers. No, let's do something that will strike sudden fear in his heart and dispose of him once and for all: Let's accept the fact that we of ourselves can do nothing. As a race of humans we've never had and never will have the power, wisdom and will to transmute this negative energy. With all the mental work we have engaged in over thousands of years to make this a better world, the results can be likened to pouring water into a swollen river. We have poured human energy into a human miscreation—which the race mind is—and bloated it even more.

The solution to the problem is to pull two plugs instead

of one. We separate ourselves from the race mind and we also break the connection with our identities as humans. We give up our mortal sense of existence with its concepts of life and death, good and evil, rich and poor, wellness and illness, peace and war, love and hate. We let it all go, wave goodbye to a human sense of being and begin our journey into the Fourth Dimension as "Non-Humans."

We do this by recognizing that on the human level we will never get out of the revolving door, and by acknowledging the greatest spiritual secret in this world: "*I of myself can do nothing.*" This is not resignation; this is POWER THINKING. As the Ageless Wisdom stated it, and later echoed by Paul, "Have nothing and you possess everything." This must be our creed if we are to gain our freedom and be all that we were created to be. I, John, cannot bring peace to this world, and neither can I feed the multitudes, heal the sick, harmonize relationships, or prosper those in the bondage of debt and limitation. No, I can't—but the Holy Master Self Who is the Reality of each one of us can.

In my opinion there are two options for humankind. One, keep on keeping on, knowing that what we do not finish this time around we will have the opportunity to do again, and again, and again, until we reach the point where the positive energy permanently outweighs the negative and our lower nature is completely transmuted.

The second approach is to come out and be separate from the human race, and in that separateness to find our oneness with God. This will not be the easiest thing to do but I believe that it is the spiritual philosophy that will be the foundation for the New World. I can say that because it was not my idea. It has been hidden in passages in all Sacred Scriptures, Ancient Wisdom Teachings and Mystical Writings, but the seeker is for the most part left to his or her own method of applying the Formula for daily living.

Clarification of Terms. Before we continue with step by step procedures, let's define some of the terms that we will be using—such as the third and fourth dimensions and the various kingdoms from the mineral to the divine. As you know, the third dimension is the plane of effect, the world of appearances, that which we perceive with our senses. It is a state of consciousness where the human kingdom is focused and includes the manifestation of the animal, plant and mineral kingdoms.

As we move into the Fourth Dimension we are lifted into omnipresence, the spiritual vibration beyond the limitations of time and space. Here we find the energy of Cause, the realm of Divine Mind, Ideas and Creative Force. It is the plane of spiritual consciousness that corresponds to the Fifth Kingdom, the Kingdom of God. Think of it this way: The fourth kingdom of the human is centered in the third dimension of effects, while the Fifth Kingdom of God operates through the Fourth Dimension of Cause.

We must also define the word "human" before we can understand what "non-human" means. First of all, "human" is a name given to something that does not exist. It is a label applied to that which is perceived to be a part of the fourth kingdom—the human kingdom—yet there is nothing written in the Akashic Records by Supreme Intelligence that says this kingdom ever existed. There is, however, an impression in the Records caused by the conscious vibrations of entities identified as those who came *from the soil*, i.e. Earthlings.

What does this mean? The significance is that the crowning glory of Creation was not a race of human beings but Beings of Light—Spiritual Beings, Divine Individuals fully ordained as Holy Ones of the Most High. Then where did humans come from? The Ancient Ones tell us that Beings of Light descended into the third-dimensional plane to experience physical matter, and they subsequently became so identified with the form side of life that spiritual consciousness was replaced by material perception. This happened over millions of years and the end result was an imprisonment of the entities in the dream state on the Earth plane.

Death and birth were two of the effects of this entrapment. Talk about a fall! Former Cosmic Conscious Beings who had full access to all dimensions were now reduced to finding release from the Earth vibration through "death"—then reentry through a physical body involving the fusion of cells by means of sexual reproduction with birth following the gestation period. This was the first instance of what we now call evolution—the evolving of cells into a physical form, all initiated and carried to fruition on the Earth plane. Thus the designation of "beings of the soil"—which is related to the Latin word *humus*, from which came *humanus*, which led to the word *human*.

It is interesting that the word *humiliate* comes from the same root word as human, and when you think about it, it is a little humiliating for Beings of the Light Realm to have to sit around and wait for the development of some fertilized egg and then to be sucked into an energy vortex to begin the process of physical growth. Anyway, as time went on an entire body of third-dimensional knowledge was created, which became the "human domain" and later glorified as the human kingdom, the fourth one up from the bottom.

And what does "non-human" mean? Simply to have a vibration in consciousness that is predominately spiritual. It means moving into the Fourth Dimension, into Omnipresence, the spiritual vibration beyond the limitation of time and space. Here you find the Energy of Cause and the Realm of Consciousness that corresponds to the Fifth Kingdom, the Kingdom of God. To the phenomenal world you appear as any other human being, but your consciousness is dramatically different. Gone are fear, reactive emotions and other undesirable aspects of personality, and in their place are the qualities of Divine Individualism. As a Being of Light you have dominion over the outer world because you are capable of expressing Fourth-Dimensional Reality into the third dimension and actually molding it according to your highest Vision—the Vision of Truth.

All is progressive, and you will find yourself moving from one level of spiritual consciousness to another, and then another, and in the process you will find greater happiness than you've ever dreamed possible.

A 60-Day Program to Transmute the Lower Energies. I challenge you now to try an experiment—to literally test the waters of the Fourth Dimension for 60 days. If you can handle the discipline, and I am sure that you can, you will find yourself living above the quicksand and roller coaster with a quality of life seldom experienced by the "human." And by the end of the test period you will scarcely remember the old you and a lifetime commitment will be made to living as the Spiritual Being you are in truth.

Here are the stages involved in the 60-day Non-Human Program:

No. 1: Establish the date that you will start the program and mark the calendar to show the duration of the two month period. A few days before you begin the program write an Agreement with your God-Self, the Holy *I* within. The purpose of the Agreement is to surrender everything that relates to your human sense of being to your Master Self. Make the statement that you are willing to give up everything on the third dimensional plane in order to have everything Fourth Dimensionally. Now when I say "give up" I am not talking about removing everything and everyone *physically*. The giving up, the releasing, the surrendering all takes place in consciousness—where it counts the most. Put your statement in writing and leave nothing out. Give up your body, your emotions, your mind. Surrender your family, friends, bank account, debts, bills—all your possessions—everything that you own in this world. The objective is to become totally detached and impersonal to your material sense of existence.

Then add to your list all your fears, needs, wants, desires, judgements, resentments, unforgiveness, jealousy, dislikes and hates. Be specific, name names, spell it out! Finally, include all positions that you have taken for or against anything or anyone, and all causes and convictions about which you feel emotional. This is an inventory of all you are and have as a human being, so keep working with the list until it is complete—*hold nothing back.*

A letter from one of the 60-day volunteers will give you an example of what it means to hold nothing back:

"I began the program with my commitment and initial meditation on letting go. My meditation was extremely powerful. I visualized a giant swirling, fiery caldron which sucked in and consumed anything that got near it. I began to release my physical possessions which one by one were devoured in the caldron. It was easy at first. Things like my car, furniture, house, workshop, bike, tools, boat, fishing gear, clothes, etc. went fairly easily and I was surprised to feel a sense of relief as they disappeared.

"When I got to behaviors and beliefs it became more difficult—I had to let go of status, position, being right, being wrong, power, control, feeling bad, feeling good, fear, strength, praise, recognition, criticism, judgements, prejudices, expectations, blame, suspicion, paranoia, hate, worry, envy, anger, sadness, and all the rest. Again, I felt a sense of relief.

"Next I got to the people closest to me—first my friends, then my brothers and sisters, my parents, my children, and finally my wife. Although this part was much more difficult, I once again felt a sense of relief and lightness as they disappeared down the caldron. I then released everything else around me and felt my own presence like I had never felt it before. I felt strong and powerful.

"As I stood there looking over the edge of the caldron I realized that the most significant and most difficult task was yet to come—letting go of my physical body and all the attachments that went with it. With great trepidation I walked to the edge of the swirling caldron and began to let go of it all—my physical strength, my appearance, physical pain, my personality, my intelligence, my abilities, being tired, responsibility, and finally my body itself. As I released my humaness, my skin and physical form peeled off and disappeared down the caldron, leaving behind an egg-shaped mass of pure energy. I felt totally free and all-knowing, totally in touch with my true self and relieved to be rid of the restrictions of physical form. "

No. 2: Now we come to the daily activities that you will follow for the two month period. Please understand that your participation in this Program does not mean that you will just "sit" for 60 days and neglect your responsibilities in the physical world. You will continue your life as before but you will be operating on a different vibration in consciousness; you will be focusing on *spirituality* rather than *materiality* and all action that you take in the outer world will be Spirit directed. Another point: if you are on medication or under the care of a doctor, do not try to break that connection until your consciousness of the Indwelling Presense as your Health has been firmly established. To continue with the points in Step 2...

• Do not pray for any material form or experience during the 60-day period. All meditation during this period must only be for a deeper realization of who and what you are. All spiritual work must be for the purpose of gaining a greater awareness, understanding and knowledge of your Master Self and a deeper recognition of the Activity of that Self.

• Agree that for 60 days your conscious mind will assume the primary role as a silent witness to the Activity of Spirit, as a beholder of the Will of God in action through you. If any desires, needs, wants or wishes come into your mind, release them quickly with the words—"*I have surrendered everything to Spirit. For 60 days I am only going to serve Spirit and not my ego. I now release the pull in my consciousness to the Christ within to be transmuted.*"

• If you are tempted to demonstrate money, health, a job, or any kind of material form, speak the word: "*I of myself can do nothing. The Spirit of God within me does the work and Spirit is doing and being everything now. My only responsibility in this matter is to abide in Spirit.''*

• Devote your meditation time to a contemplation of your Holy Self. Ponder the infinite Knowingness of that Self—Its Wisdom and Intelligence. Meditate on Its Life, Love, Joy and Power. Feel and sense the incredibly creative energy radiating from the Infinite Mind within and focus on what this energy represents. Be aware that it is the very Thought Energy of God embodying perfect Thoughtforms of abundance, wholeness, harmony, protection, peace, right relations, right action, divine order, divine guidance, and the substance of all physical forms and experiences.

See the flow as the invisible Kingdom of Spirit and put yourself right in the middle of that Kingdom—not as a human being but as an individualized Energy Field of Spirit—as a Spiritual Being, and see every detail of your Fourth Dimensional life as absolutely perfect. Keep your mind off the form and on the inner invisible world of harmony, wholeness and omnipresent non-material supply. For 60 days you are going to operate in the spiritual realm where no physical structure exists. You are going to keep your thoughts off of "this world" and on the ideas of Energy, Life, Love, Light, Essence, Mind— the *invisible* world of Spirit.

• As you go about your day keep these thoughts in mind when lower (ego) promptings come through:

I do not need to pray for a soulmate relationship. The perfect relationship for me already exists in the Master Mind within. I need only to identify and recognize my Spirit as the Source and Activity of all my relationships and spiritual law will work through my consciousness to reveal the perfect complement to my soul. I no longer have the responsibility for finding my right mate.

I do not need to demonstrate money for my Holy Self embodies all the abundance of the universe. I already have everything that I could possibly desire right now. The I that I AM is the Spirit of Infinite Plenty in action and my role is to simply be aware of the prospering power of God taking place in and through me. I have turned over the management of my financial affairs to Spirit, and I let the Law of Spirit manifest as my all-sufficiency. I no longer have any concern about money.

I do not have to treat metaphysically for a healthy body, for the Self that I AM is eternally whole and perfect. My consciousness of this Truth is my Health, so I quit paying so much attention to my physical form. I place my focus on the Presence of God I AM and the invisible Energy Field that is my Divine Body. Spirit is the Energy of all form and I let Spirit form Its physical structure as It sees fit. This physical body is no longer any of my business.

I will not be concerned about that project that is before me to do since I'm not the one who will be doing it. The Master within is perfectly aware of what's to be done, and by keeping my mind stayed on the Presence, Spirit will work through my awareness to accomplish everything easily, effortlessly and creatively. I don't have to get uptight about anything anymore.

I will not worry about this planet and all of the appearances that I read and hear about. My Holy Self is omnipresent which means that there is no place on Earth where Spirit is not. This Spirit of God embodies all peace, love, joy, right relations, right action, and I let my awareness of this Truth be the channel for the healing and harmonizing of all conditions. This world is in God's Hands and is no longer any of my concern.

Do you see what you are doing with this way of thinking, feeling and seeing? You are separating yourself from the race mind that thinks, feels and sees only third-dimensionally. You are coming out from under the creature who knows only the physical and material aspects of life, and in doing so you are allowing Spirit, rather than the collective consciousness, to express as form and experience in your world. But to make this program work you must give up concern about anything and everything, knowing that through your awareness of the indwelling Presence all things within the range of your consciousness are adjusted, harmonized, healed, prospered and protected. And when emotional charges are set off in your system and "Oh-Lord-what-will-I-do?" thoughts come into your mind, just stop right there and say:

This is none of my business. Those red flags were for my human self and it does not exist anymore. I am a spiritual being living in a spiritual universe as a witness to the Activity of God, and I refuse to descend back into the dense vibrations to fight the battle. I've given everything to Spirit and now I have everything spiritually—and this spiritual energy is now revealing the Finished Kingdom. I am free at last!

No. 3: Begin each day, even before you get out of bed, by expressing loving gratitude for all the good in your life, for the everywhere present Activity of God. Even the most destitute and desperate can always find something to be thankful about and this you must do for it is of critical importance. By daily "counting your blessings" a vibration of love and joy will begin to move through your consciousness calling for all the good in your life to grow and multiply. Remember that gratitude not only eliminates negative patterns caused by ingratitude, but it also works with the Law of Attraction to bring to you that which has already been tagged with your name, i.e. the good that your Spirit has already manifested for your "life more abundant" but which your lower vibration has repelled.

If you will truly dedicate yourself to living as a *spiritual being* for the full 60 days, you just might wake up one morning and find that you are living in the Fourth Dimension...on an Island of Light where everything that you could possibly desire is already in perfect expression as form and experience...and Truth is your eternal shield.

The Promises for Those Who Walk in the Light.

Throughout the Scriptures and sacred writings we read of trials and tribulations coming to this world, and in each passage there is always a condition, which if met, will provide refuge and safety. Look at the 91st Psalm as an example. It says, "He that dwelleth in the secret place of the Most High shall abide under the shadow of the Almighty."

Notice that it says *dwelleth*, which means to live, inhabit, abide—and not to run in when things look tough and run out when everything seem rosy. The result of this staying in one place? "He shall deliver thee from the snare of the fowler and from the noisome pestilence...he shall cover thee with his feathers...his truth shall be thy shield and buckler...a thousand shall fall at thy side and ten thousand at thy right hand, but it shall not come nigh thee...there shall no evil befall thee, neither shall any plague come nigh thy dwelling."

Now there's a significance to all those bodies being piled up at your feet. It is a graphic way of saying that people simply cannot be protected if they are not in the spiritual vibration. In "mortal consciousness" one plays the law of averages and partakes of the game of chance. In spiritual consciousness "the dice of God are always loaded" in favor of those dwelling in the Secret Place.

And the 46th Psalm promises the same thing..."God is our refuge..." In other words, when we abide in the consciousness of Spirit we find shelter. By finding our refuge within, in the one Presence and Power of our being, we are protected even though "the earth be removed and the mountains carried into the midst of the sea...though the waters roar and be troubled, though the mountains shake with swelling."

The promises are there for those who walk in the Light, and we could not ask for more because we cannot violate spiritual law—the Law of Consciousness. *It shall be done unto you according to the state of your consciousness.*

Before the first World Healing Day on December 31, 1986, I asked my Self, "What if disinterest and ignorance hold sway and there is no optimum participation?" Here is the answer I received: "Through the efforts of millions of men and women with purity of motive and a consciousness reaching for Christhood, the world of illusion will separate into islands of Light and darkness. Those attracted to the Light will gather as one, offering their hearts and minds, their love and will, to the Eternal Light...and they shall be taken into the Light and they shall become the Light. And the Light shall spread to the island of darkness...and it will cease to exist. And from the Island of Light a new Earth and a new Civilization will emerge."

I feel that everyone on the planet benefits to some extent anytime even one individual moves into the Christ Consciousness because we are all one in the omnipresence of Spirit. And we can help those who continue to walk in the darkness through an expansion and a deepening of our own spiritual vibrations. So it does begin with individual you and me and the millions of others on this planet who are working spiritually for an end to the sense of separation.

The bottom line is that each one of us must seek and find and know our Holy Self and let Spirit do the rest through our meditations and uplifted consciousness. We must become detached from appearance, knowing that whatever happens in the phenomenal world is simply consciousness in expression—providing safety and protection for those in the Light and learning experiences for those who remain in the darkness.

CHAPTER 2

Consciousness and the Kingdom

If you have accepted my challenge and are participating in the 60-day non-human program, you have made an inventory in writing of all that you are and have as a human being and have surrendered all to the Holy Self within. For some of you this releasing activity may have been a highly sacred ceremony with great meaning and intensity, and after giving up everything on the list you burned the paper and scattered the ashes. And you are repeating the process, daily if necessary, to eliminate any new physical/material pulls not uncovered in the original inventory.

Continuing with the daily program you are becoming impersonal and detached to the mental-emotional drain of the material world and are focusing intently on the spiritual Presence within, seeking only a greater awareness of the Master Self and a deeper recognition of the Activity of that Self. And in the process, consciousness is changing, expanding, rising, separating itself from the vampirism of the race mind and taking on the spiritual vibration of the Fifth Kingdom. You are realizing the significance of *Consciousness as Cause*. Let's take a closer look at what this means.

What is Consciousness? Consciousness is the balance sheet revealing the sum total of all your thoughts, emotions and realizations registered during all your lives on Planet Earth. It includes your assets, liabilities, and spiritual net worth as an individual—all vibrating to a particular tone and pitch. Within this individualized Energy Field called *you* is an imprint of all that you have done and all that has been done to you. There are subconscious pockets of pulsating memories of all the good that you have brought into this world—and the energy of fear, hate, greed, guilt, cruelty and depravity are there, too, unless they have been transmuted through payment of karmic debts or realizations of Truth.

Your thinking mind is not your consciousness; your thoughts feed your consciousness and it is the trend of your thoughts and emotions that shapes your consciousness. Consciousness is your awareness, understanding and knowledge about everything that has been a part of your individual experience. And until you pursue the level of Christ or Cosmic Consciousness, this particular energy vibration that you are remains a part of the collective consciousness, which is the sum total of the mental-emotional experience of humanity.

For the ''human'' being, consciousness is the pattern through which the Light-Substance-Energy of God flows to create in the physical world that which corresponds to the individual's dominant vibration. The Ancients described this as consciousness ''not in control.'' The effect produced in the outer world matches not only the person's belief system, but also the race mind beliefs that have been unconsciously accepted under the hypnotic spell of mortality.

Does consciousness have power? For the unawakened, it functions as the outlet through which creative energy flows into form and experience, i.e. it works as an effect to produce a like effect. Yet, we can say that consciousness has power, under law, to express itself.

As we move up into higher levels of consciousness, a sense of mastery (control) dawns in us and we begin to consciously cooperate with the Source within. We move from religious fallen man/woman into experimental metaphysics and on up to practical mysticism where the spiritual faculties are opened and we, as Consciousness, become Cause to our world. This is Consciousness *in control*, the Consciousness of Dominion.

To summarize, we know that if consciousness is focused exclusively on the outer world of form, the creative energy released will be totally conditioned by *human* consciousness which includes the universal belief that "if anything can go wrong it will." It is a belief system that says that good is subservient to evil; that light can be overcome by darkness; that accidents, sickness, lack, failure and conflict are the natural order of things. However, we also know that if consciousness is predominantly spiritual, the energy expressed will be from the Mind of God within, which manifests as harmlessness, wholeness, abundance, fulfillment and harmony. So we have a choice—to live as a human being, or as a spiritual being.

Do you see now why we all must give up our sense of humanhood? Do you understand why we must accept the truth that in a state of human consciousness we can do nothing? Have you realized that only by giving up the material sense of existence, by surrendering all attachments on the third-dimensional plane, can we ever manifest the Kingdom on Earth?

The Kingdom Defined. The four kingdoms on the third dimensional plane are the mineral, plant, animal and human. The Fifth Kingdom is the realm of Harmony, or Heaven. It is the Spiritual Consciousness of the Fourth Dimension. To live in the Fifth Kingdom means to experience, right here in physical form on a physical planet, all of the attributes of the spiritual plane. It means that the Circle of Life that you call *your* individual world will be a manifestation of *Love*. Now imagine what a world— *your world*—created out of the Energy of Love would be like. Could there possibly be any lack, limitation or insufficiency? No. Could there possibly be harmfulness in any area? No.

Capture the vision of what this means. A world reflecting a spiritual consciousness would be awesomely beautiful. Nature would have a different look as the lower kingdoms sing together in joyful harmony—and your immediate environment would reflect divine order, peace and goodwill. Your body would feel youthful, strong, and cooperative. Your feeling nature would be lifted to new heights of love, joy, gratitude and contentment, and your mind would dwell in the currents of constructive power and creative action for the greatest good of all.

In no time you would realize that you have an all-sufficiency of visible supply to meet every need and live life more abundantly. You would also notice that the people attracted into your immediate world are gentle, loving, and helpful in every way. And soon, if you are not already in your true place, you would find yourself moved into the perfect opportunity to experience joyful fulfillment in your work. Even with all of this glorious good surrounding you, you would know that you as a thinking, reasoning personality had nothing to do with it. You were simply a witness to a rather hellish kind of existence being replaced with a heavenly environment—without you even taking thought except to be **AWARE** of the Truth of your being. How do you find and move into that Kingdom which is your true estate? Let's find the answer.

The New World of the Fifth Kingdom. First of all, we must understand that the Fifth Kingdom of God is a Finished Kingdom already existing in the invisible, and that it comes forth into manifestation as a radiation of individual consciousness. This Kingdom of Harmony is the Real World, the New World—"new" to our human experience. In truth, it has always existed as the Will, Plan and Purpose of That Which we call Supreme Being, or God. This "other world" in which most of us presently live is the collective consciousness made manifest, and it has been called an illusion because it is temporary, not permanent, thus not real.

Yet both the Real World and the world of shadows are an outpicturing of consciousness. One is our human concept of reality projected on the third dimensional screen of life, and the other is the Truth of Reality projected on the same screen. Everything on the "screen" is an effect, from the physical body to the physical universe, and the cause of these effects is *consciousness*. The effect can be a humanly-conceived appearance or a God-conceived Reality—depending on the state, level, vibration of consciousness.

When Jesus said, "My Kingdom is not of this world," he was explaining that Spiritual Reality must not be confused with appearances—that "this world" was not created or outpictured by Spiritual Consciousness which he represented, but by the mortal consciousness of the race mind, universal or individualized.

Now we see one signpost on the path leading to the Kingdom. It reads: *"Attempt not to change that which has been created by man, but let Consciousness reveal that which has been created by God."* We could also say that you cannot change the motion picture from the audience. You must go to the projector, which is consciousness, and change the film. The point here is that if you attempt to fix, change or heal a third-dimensional effect with a third-dimensional consciousness, all you are doing is repairing a fake wall with fake plaster. It might look good for a time but sooner or later it is going to fall apart again. Now let's look at more signposts on the path.

"You of yourself can do nothing, and God's work is already completed, so where does that leave you? It leaves you with a priceless gift on which the future of humanity rests: Consciousness." We must all reach the point where we understand that humans, using the mortal mind as power, can only continue to build the scenery, paint the drops, arrange the props and play the role in the amateur playhouse productions on earth. And we must also realize that God's Kingdom is finished and was pronounced "Very Good." But the Almighty didn't just say "It is done" and leave it at that. The next step was to give the Kingdom and "all that the Father has" to the Holy High Self, the **I**

33

AM of each individual being. Thus the Will, Plan and Purpose of God—for the individual and the world—was planted in consciousness under the care and supervision of the Christ within, the Spirit of Individuality, with these instructions: ''Let the Kingdom radiate like the rays of the sun; let it flow like a mighty river, to be manifest in the visible world in accordance with the unfoldment of consciousness.''

What does this mean? Let's find the answer in this meditation:

Spirit of the Living God within, my precious Reality, I have given up everything, surrendered all to you, and now I come before you as a spiritual child seeking only the Kingdom.

I know now that you are the keeper of the Kingdom and that you love me so much that it is your good pleasure to give me, your joint heir, the fullness of this sacred Gift. I now open my entire awareness of being to receive the radiant rays and the mighty flow.

I feel the infilling. Oh God I feel it! Throughout my being I am experiencing the pouring in of Divine Substance, Light, Love, the radiant Essence of Mind, the infinite Supply of the whole Kingdom of God. I am being filled, filled, filled...my cup runneth over. My mind and heart are saturated and permeated and overflowing with the creative Thought-Energy of God, the Divine Thoughtforms of the Fifth Kingdom.

The invisible Kingdom has come. The Lord's Prayer has been fulfilled. I am now the Kingdom Consciousness, and I know that I now possess all that I could ever need or desire for all eternity. I am now ready for the Invisible Kingdom to be manifest in the visible world of form. I now consent to the expression on Earth of the Will, Plan and Purpose of God.

It is happening now. Look! The Kingdom is radiating from my Consciousness like the rays of the sun, flowing like a mighty river. The Divine Thoughtforms are being projected into visibility. I see this...I feel it.

Where there was loneliness and emptiness there is now love and fullness of companionship. I see this...I feel it.

Where there was lack and limitation there is now abundance. I see this...I feel it.

Where there was illness there is now wellness. I see this...I feel it.

Where there was conflict there is now peace. I see this...I feel it.

Where there was sorrow there is now joy. I see this...I feel it.

Where there was a human sense of being there is now the spiritual livingness in the Kingdom of God—my Kingdom on Earth. I see this...I feel it...and it is so!

As you continue your 60-day program, please remember these points:

1. Surrender every pull, concern, worry, attachment, need—everything that represents your concept of living in the physical world—release it all to the Spirit within. Do this daily if necessary.

2. Continue to be active in the world but not as a fearful, anxious human. Keep your mind stayed on the **I AM**, your Divine Consciousness, knowing that anything happening "out there" is none of your business.

3. When blips come up, use the statements of truth presented in Chapter One. Remember that you cannot live on yesterday's manna (energy). Rising out of human-hood is a daily process.

4. Instead of praying for things and conditions, ponder the invisible Allness that is already yours within.

5. Contemplate the Truth that the activity of Spirit is the eternal givingness of the Kingdom, and within the Kingdom is the fulfillment of every need and desire.

6. Use the meditation in this chapter each day until it "takes." *Feel* the action taking place, but in your visualization ("I see this") do not outline how the Divine Thoughtforms are to manifest. Just see the joyful completion—"the happy ending."

7. Keep the idea of the Kingdom within you fully present in your consciousness. Think about it continuously throughout the day with great love.

Can Peace Come to a World Created by the Collective Consciousness?

As I was writing the material for this second chapter I had a deep realization in consciousness that went far beyond intellectual awareness. It was when I first wrote that an illusion is "only temporary, not permanent, thus not real" that I had a flow-through of ideas with continuity that provided greater insight on the two worlds. This was not a "channeled" message but rather an impression from the Higher Nature within. It said:

"The world you see through human eyes is the collective mind objectified. It is only a temporary world wholly vulnerable to the Energy of Change, which may be called the destroyer aspect of Divinity, not in the sense of retribution but a joyful correcting to fulfill the Law of Harmony.

"This present world as you perceive it is a stage of sight and sound that must be struck to reveal the world of God's Vision. The effects cannot be attacked, however. The process must begin in mind to separate itself from the source of pain, and as the source of this world is removed, so must the effects.

"Understand that that which is changeable, unstable,

volatile must obey the mandate of transmutation—and that which can be changed will be changed, by spiritual law. An illusion cannot be healed; it can either be replaced with another false image, or it can be removed and replaced with reality.

"The world is out of focus. It is a blur of delusion, a darkened fog, a mirror of fear and unforgiveness. Through the Light the world is being brought into focus. As the mirror concentrates the Light Waves, Holy Fire becomes manifest, consuming that which is passing and impermanent and melting the mask to reveal a world seen through the eyes of Christ Consciousness.

"The Healing Light that ignites this Holy Fire is within all, thus each can be the Revealer, for the Light is omnipresent—yet the Fire is present only where focused. Will you be a Revealer? You seek peace on Earth, but it will not be manifest in the fog of insanity. It is an effect of the Kingdom of Love which issues forth from those who abandon ego and seek only the Way and Truth of Spirit.

"The manifestation of the Kingdom of Love is Light. As the Light touches the mirror of distortion the focused Light produces Fire to destroy the illusion. As the smoke clears the Kingdom is revealed, which is peace on Earth within the sphere of the Revealers.

"Where does this happen? In mind, in consciousness. The world of illusion that you see is within you. The Kingdom of God is within you. The radiation takes place within you. The convergence of Light and Fire happens within you, and the revelation of the Kingdom takes place within you. The entire transmutation process takes place within, within consciousness, and then behold, all things are made new.

"The New World can only be seen through the eyes of the spiritually minded, for what they see is an outer symbol of the inner consciousness. Likewise, the world of insanity can only be seen through the eyes of the mortal minded, for what they see is an outer symbol of the inner consciousness. Both worlds will co-exist until the collective mind is fully Christed. Those living in the shadows will experience the fate of the shadows; those living in the Light will experience the freedom of the Radiance—yet all takes place within the invisible realm of mind, and what is seen in the respective worlds is but an extension of mind.

"Where is poverty, hunger, disease? In the mind of delusion. Where are international conflict, war and destruction? In the mind of delusion. Where do upheavals in nature take place? In that same mind. These effects are visible symbols of the insanity of that state of consciousness.

"Where is the Peace of God and the total harmony that this peace represents? In the Consciousness of Truth, a mind stayed on God, a Spiritual Mind. Is a Spiritual Mind vulnerable to the world of shadows? No, unless it chooses to descend from Light into darkness. Can a totally *human* mind partake of the Kingdom? No, because it does not know that it exists. However, in an instant of sanity a decision can be made to seek the Light—and with each degree of understanding a greater clarity comes into mind, leading the individual into the Light and revealing the nothingness of the darkness.

"There are written and spoken prophecies stating that the winds of destruction are upon humankind and offering the view that after the final cleansing, peace will prevail on Earth. This is a scenario that can certainly take place within the world of shadows but not in the World of Light."

After contemplating the above information over a period of days I began to think of the meaning and significance of the Planetary Commission and World Healing Day. The objective of the Annual Global Mind-Link is to reverse the polarity of the negative force field and achieve a critical mass of positive energy, insuring a chain reaction of self-sustaining Good in the world. Do you see now that this must happen in consciousness first—that the healing of the world is a healing of consciousness, which then reveals the New World?

The Commission members throughout the world must be the Revealers—men, women and children who have moved out from under the race mind and are radiating the Kingdom Energies to melt the mask. Our mission is not to heal the illusion but to remove it and replace it with reality.

When many people with an uplifted spiritual consciousness are gathered together (in mind) with a single purpose, the power is multiplied extraordinarily. A giant Energy Field, a massive Thoughtform, is created. A unified consciousness of spiritually-minded Light Workers emerges, which then dissolves the "old world"—no, no—not the form, but the *idea of the world within the consciousness of the group Energy Field*. Then what is seen "out there" reflects that Consciousness. But if we focus on the physical world, on the effects projected by the race mind and attempt to manipulate matter and change the appearances, we will fail. The world will still be the same as it was in consciousness with only a few temporary positive adjustments on the world scene to provide a sense of hope.

Efforts to heal every manifestation of insanity in the visible world slam right up against the insane collective consciousness producing those effects, and the dramatic changes sought will not be evident. However, through the Global Mind-Link we are creating Islands of the Kingdom where peace and harmony prevail. And with each mighty thrust into the race mind another Island appears, and then another, "and the Light shall spread to the island of darkness, and it shall cease to exist"—for the mortal consciousness will have been transmuted and "a new Earth and a new Civilization will emerge."

CHAPTER 3

The Kingdom Energies of Radiation and Attraction

It is a Universal Law that you always experience your consciousness. If you are not experiencing harmony and wholeness in your life, it is because your consciousness is not yet harmonious and whole. We are what we are. We always express the "self" that we are living, and what we radiate *as* that self is attracted back to us. Nothing is by chance; everything is based on principle.

To give up the idea of humanhood simply means that we stop living a life of constant *reaction*—reacting to effects and outer stimulus with fear, anger, depression and futility. Who created those situations in the first place? We did, by the vibrations of our consciousness. How do we change those vibrations? By embodying the Kingdom— the Divine Consciousness that is *already* the Reality of us.

In the previous chapter we talked about the Kingdom—the God **I AM** Consciousness that includes all the Divine Thoughtforms *eternally in action* to fulfill the Law of Harmony in each individual's world. We know that a law of nature says that water seeks its own level. It has to. It has no choice in the matter because it is an unbreakable law. And the same thing holds true with the Law of Harmony. It is impossible to live a life of anything less than perfect harmony, which includes serenity, joy, love, wellness, abundance, right relations, protection and divine order. That's the Law!

But wait a minute. If that's the Law, why are so many people up to their arm pits in quicksand? Go back to the law that says water seeks its own level. The law is in effect *only* if there is water. If there is no water to seek its own level, the law does not apply. Similarly, without a spiritual consciousness, life does not conform to the absolute rule of harmony. To put it another way, to live the idea of humanhood places us under the influence of a third-dimensional law—the Law of Incongruity where life is at variance with Truth.

I have also pointed out that ''for the great majority of humankind, consciousness is the pattern through which the Light-Substance-Energy of God flows to create in the physical world that which corresponds to the individual's dominant vibration''—saying that this was consciousness ''not in control.'' Think about that again. The identity that you are living always goes before you to create the experience of that identity because the energy flowing through you *assumes that identity*! This is another way of describing the Law of Correspondence. The *idea* that you are human creates human experiences; the *Idea* that you are a Spiritual Being creates spiritual experiences in the physical world, which is the meaning of ''in Earth as it is in Heaven.''

You must dismiss completely from your mind the idea that a spiritual life on Planet Earth is boring, tedious, unfulfilling, sacrificing, and blessedly poor. When the Divine Thoughtforms are expressed on the physical plane through you, your life becomes complete in every area—with joy and happiness, serenity and peace reigning supreme. Just remember that being spiritual and being religious are not necessarily the same. Spirituality is the focus on the Reality *within*, on the Light, Love and Life of the emerging Master, a thrilling adventure of awakening to the glory you had in the beginning. Religiosity on the other hand is usually a focus on the *without*, with observances, beliefs and practices per-

sonifying fear, guilt and individual repression—thus emphasizing humanhood and strengthening the sense of
separation.

By-passing the humanhood vibration. A few years ago I
became very frustrated with the metaphysical idea that I
was a victim of my own consciousness. (You did it, John.
Don't blame anyone but you.) I knew that my problems
were an outpicturing of what was going on inside of me,
and I knew that as soon as the positive vibrations out-
weighed the negative my outer world would begin to
change. But good Lord, how long would it take? I was
willing to do my part, but I also expected a little help from
Spirit—not to turn stones into dollars or nasty clients into
loving ones—but to help me change my consciousness.
That's the least God could do, I thought.

Within a relatively short time I received an answer. A
new understanding said that I had a choice of either
expressing self or Self. If I wanted to express my lower
nature, all I had to do was keep my mind stayed on the
world of effects, and my reaction to those effects would
signal the impersonal law to create more of the same.
Conversely, if I wanted to express the Truth of Being, my
role in the scheme of things was to be *conscious of the
Master Self within,* and this action of being aware would
channel the Divine Energy through that awareness. It
was too simple to believe at first, too easy to be a stepping
stone to mastery. After all, aren't things metaphysical
and mystical supposed to be difficult and complicated? I
thought so, but I took the easy way out and began a
program of practicing Self-awareness—just being alert
and mindful that my Christ Self was where I was, right
where I felt alive and loving. After a few so-called
miracles occurred in my life, I realized what I was doing.
I was giving the radiating energy an identity idea, not a
realization yet, just an *idea.* And this idea was diverting
the energy away from the programmed patterns in consciousness and channeling it through a thoughtform that
corresponded more to the true nature of the energy.

The Searchlight of the Soul. When the creative energy radiates through your conscious awareness of the Holy I within, it creates experiences that correspond to that Self. Later it came to me that the Master Self is like a giant searchlight shining in all directions eternally radiating the All Good, and that I could consciously cooperate with my Self (in addition to being Self-aware) by practicing the technique of *radiation*—radiating the attributes of the Master Self, particularly those that seemed to be missing in my life. As I did this amazing things began to happen.

Let's pause for a moment to get the feel of *radiating*. Get still and quiet, become conscious of the Presence in and around you, and with a focus of will and love begin to radiate *your awareness of Spirit*. Say the following words and feel the dynamic radiation of energy—then see with the inner eye this energy as light filling your world.

I am radiating, with intensity, my conscious awareness of my Divine Self.

I am radiating, with intensity, the Joy of my Divine Self.

I am radiating, with intensity, the Wholeness of my Divine Self.

I am radiating, with intensity, the Abundance of my Divine Self.

Practice the idea of radiating from the level of Soul...practice until you get the feel of being a giant searchlight, a mighty sun, and keep practicing daily until the action is instinctive and spontaneous.

Radiation establishes the magnetic field. During a later mediation a flow through of thoughts said, *"I go before you to adjust according to the Divine Standard those things where direct action on your part is not required. This is only a part of my work, however. The primary thrust of my activity is through your livingness AS me, for then I am in control of your immediate environment. The I and the Kingdom are one...they cannot be separated. When you embody one you embody the other. When you radiate your Self-awareness you are radiating* *the Divine Ideas of the Kingdom. When the lower nature is completely under the control of the Higher, you will experience seemingly instant manifestation. Until then, the good you seek will be attracted to you as the radiation establishes a magnetic field around you.''*

This communication contributed more to my understanding of how Spirit works on the physical plane than anything in a long while. Until we can manifest form and experience right out of substance, our good is *attracted* to us. The people, events, situations, conditions, and circumstances that correspond to our Self-awareness are brought to us through the Law of Attraction. And that Law goes into effect through the radiation process. What we radiate through our conscious awareness of the Master Self within comes back to us multiplied and overflowing. So we see that Spirit not only goes before us, through radiation, to level mountains, but is also eternally with us to fulfill every need through attraction.

Let's pause again and this time experience the feeling of being a *magnet* for our good. Simply be still and see-feel that radiating light as it begins to attract, drawing to you the All-Good from the far corners of the universe. Feel the radiation and the magnetic power working simultaneously. Keep practicing this exercise until you feel the energies of radiation and attraction working together and the action is automatic in your consciousness. This will be important later when we begin to consciously work as Cause to our world.

I of myself can do nothing. Now let's go back and look at the human sense of being again. What does a human being think about most of the time? Lack, limitation, unfulfillment, disease, disorder, death, the possibility of this and the probability of that, the law of averages, and on and on. All of these ideas blend into one of self-identification because the human identifies all of these ideas with his or her own experience. And guess what? That which you live *as* you live *with*. But what happens when we fully commit to the idea that ''I of myself can do nothing"? The mind shifts to encompass that which can do *something*, for the universe cannot tolerate inaction. The mind seeks a power, the presence of authority, to take the place of the I that can do nothing. To use a word that the Jews at that time could understand, a word that would command obedience, Jesus said—"It is the *Father* within who doeth the works."

Who/What is the fathering principle? You are! The Spiritual You, the Master I, the Holy Self. The individualization of God that you are in truth is the ONE who protects, prospers, heals, arranges, adjusts, and makes all things new. To emphasize the significance of this permit me to share another revelation with you.

For years I searched and explored the deepest recesses of my being looking for God. I knew that I could not transcend my humanhood until I changed my consciousness from mortal to spiritual, and I figured that the only way to do this was to find God, become consciously aware of the Presence and establish a meaningful relationship with the Almighty. And so I "carried my lamp" into the darkness of my mind and heart—constantly pushing, pressing, clawing and scratching for a glimmer of this Being called Supreme. Then one day I heard the words: *"Know Thyself! Seek not the Great Unknown but recognize your Self as God in expression, closer than life, only a thought away in consciousness."*

I have heard this admonition three times...first in the 1970's, then later when I was writing *The Planetary Commission*, and again after we formally commenced the 60-day non-human program. The analogies that came to mind each time were numerous, such as looking for my glasses only to find that I was wearing them, becoming aware of the inside of the shirt I had on, or the sudden remembrance of a friend whom I had not thought about in years. And then it dawned on me. The God that I was looking for was that part of my very own consciousness that was spiritual. The object of my search was not an Entity separate from me; the seeking was for a part of *me* just beyond the range of my senses. It wasn't Something apart from me; it was Me, Myself, I—the Spirit of God made manifest as my very own Divine Consciousness. I decided to accept the Truth that *I* was *It*—not my conscious mind but a higher level of Mind "only a thought away in consciousness." With the inner eye I saw that formless Self and realized that I could feel this God-Self by feeling Life within me, *as* me, and by feeling the incredible power of love surging through me. A thousand burdens lifted from my shoulders because now I had Something tangible and as close as breathing to commune with—not a far off unapproachable God but a living, loving Presence that is the Reality of *my* Being.

But even with this greater understanding of my Self I seemed to remain in the pig pen, and so I asked—"What about this little me who sees incompleteness, sorrow and suffering in the world and personally wallows in negative emotions?" And the voice said, *"That is not a part of you. It is simply the energy of the mind-aggregate, as beliefs, flowing through receptive centers in tune with the lower vibration. They are but beliefs which will in time be dissolved by the One who does not believe but only Knows. As the beliefs are dissolved the personality is not destroyed. Rather, the lower nature is taken over by the Christ Aspect and the human person resumes identity as a Spiritual Individual. This is Divine Individualism."*

In pondering these ideas the thought came to mind that a "human" is really not an individual at all. It is really a massive thoughtform made up of the thoughts of incarnates of all ages as they fearfully reacted to the effects of their own miscreations. It is an energy mass that hovers around the planet seeking an entrance into consciousness, and those who embody that energy are called "human." And that understanding helped even more in the flight to freedom.

Review of where we are.

1. We began by surrendering everything in our lives that relates to a human sense of being, giving all to the Spirit within. We made the commitment to become totally

detached to lack, debt, ailments, possessions, conditions and situations in our individual worlds. We cut the cord on people, places and things that caused pulls in our consciousness, and we put our emotions under control of the Higher Self so that all resentment, condemnation, judgement, unforgiveness and jealousy would be transmuted. We gave up causes and stopped being against anything, knowing that what is going on ''out there'' is none of our business.

2. We consented to embark on a 60-day experiment where all meditation, prayer and treatments would be only for a deeper realization of the Master Self within and a greater recognition of the Activity of that Self. Knowing that we of ourselves could do nothing, we decided to let go of humanhood and trust Spirit with everything.

3. We have meditated on receiving the Kingdom in consciousness, and then radiated the Kingdom like rays of the sun, seeing it flow like a mighty river, and we began to feel a new spiritual sense of being.

4. We are keeping our mind on the Holy Self within to by-pass the humanhood vibration, radiating the energy of this Self-awareness and becoming a magnet for the All-Good as it is attracted into our lives.

5. We are realizing the Presence of God, not reaching for the Unattainable but understanding how The Great Unknown IS expresses from the formless and individualizes as our very own SELF—only a thought away in consciousness.

6. And in the whole process we are experiencing a freedom not known before, as we are getting the lower natures out of the way and letting Spirit manifest the Kingdom on Earth through us, as us.

A Contemplative Meditation.

I am invisible, for Spirit is invisible and I am Spirit.

I am invisible, for Cause is invisible and I am Cause.

I am invisible, for Soul is invisible and I am Soul.

I am invisible, for Consciousness is invisible and I am Consciousness.

I am invisible, for Body is invisible and I am Body.

I am invisible, therefore, in prayer and meditation I seek that which is invisible, for to seek form is contrary to my nature.

I am invisible, therefore my supply is invisible, for it is substance, the pure essence of my Consciousness.

I am invisible, and to judge that which is seen is to decree lack and limitation, for what is seen is but an infinitesimal fragment of that which infinitely is.

I am invisible, and so is my love, wisdom, power, health, abundance, peace, harmony, joy, and the essence of my relationships.

I am invisible. As my consciousness of the invisible Activity of Spirit expands, the greater and grander will be the manifestations in my life, for the invisible Cause is infinite and the forms eternally unlimited, yet that which is seen in mind as finite is forever limited in visible expression.

I am invisible.

CHAPTER 4

Living the Attributes of the Master Self

In learning how to *live* and *be* a Fourth Dimensional Being on the third dimensional plane, we should take another quick look at the Dracula connection.

In *The Superbeings* I said that behind all fiction was a basis for truth, and the Dracula literature is no exception. If we consider Dracula as representing the deviant energy of the race mind that draws its power from individual energy fields, we begin to understand that "evil" is the energy of miscreation functioning as a vampire. Now, in Dracula folklore, who was the prime target? Women, symbolizing the Mother Substance of creation. And where was the point of attack? The throat, representing the organ of creative power.

Do you see the significance in this symbolism? The malevolent force in the mind-aggregate forever seeks to sustain the Dream by maintaining individual consciousness in the lowest possible vibration. It does this by drawing on the Life Force of creative expression emanating from the individual's energy field, thus decelerating and ultimately blocking the creative process. "Creative" as we are using it here refers to the creative purpose of the Soul in its evolutionary movement toward full awakening of personal consciousness. So again we see our objective: To come out and be separate from the race mind and regain our Identities as Spiritual Beings.

In Chapter Three we talked about by-passing the humanhood vibration through Self-awareness. We also discussed the radiation of the conscious awareness of Self, and the Law of Attraction that corresponds to our Self Identification. Let's continue now with a discussion of how to *live* the attributes of the Master within and *be* the creative expression of that Self, which will protect our energy field and the evolutionary process of the Soul. And one of the major keys in this process is *harmlessness*.

Ageless Wisdom tells us that there is a lower and higher form of harmlessness—the higher being perfect, a dynamic energy which cannot as yet be handled by humans. However, the lower aspect of harmlessness, which is in itself a transforming power, can be practiced by the human family as a means of escaping from the race mind influence.

There are three basic requirements in attaining the harmlessness state of mind, each of which can be interpreted on any rung of the evolutionary ladder. For our purposes here we will look at the requirements from the standpoint of an aspirant rather than a master. They are:

1. Poise — the ability to control the emotions while fully expressing spiritual feelings...to be free from reactions to disturbances in the outer world while simultaneously being joyfully loving. It means cutting the cords and eliminating the pulls on everything that makes you feel less than a gloriously alive and happy spiritual being. It is the practice of "Divine Indifference" while maintaining a deep feeling of unconditional love.

2. Detached Observation — to observe with unconditional love and discernment the activities of the phenomenal world *as if you were not a part of that world*. This is assuming the role of the beholder. You witness the Law of Cause and Effect in operation as you see individuals and groups sow and reap from many levels of consciousness—from the grossest to the finest. You observe all without judgement, not labeling anything good or bad.

3. Spiritual Understanding — to recognize that Self-awareness is a consciousness functioning as an open channel for the spiritual energy of Divine Mind, and knowing that this energy will transmute understanding from human to spiritual. You become a mind aware of its SELF, holding steady in the radiating Light of that Self, ready to participate in the action of Self according to the understanding and guidance received.

When we are practicing harmlessness we are free to live as the Master Self, for we have entered a state of mind where goodwill is the motive behind all activity. And in this consciousness, which is constantly aware of the Presence within, we are in creative action to reveal the Good Will of God. This may mean firm action, sometimes even considered drastic to humans in the nightmare, but we cannot *be* spiritual beings without *living* the Truth. Let's look at some examples in case there is any confusion at this point.

If someone comes to you for help and speaks of insufficiency, hard times, poor relationships, illness, etc., can you be divinely indifferent? Can you be lovingly detached? Can you hold your mind in the Light of spiritual understanding regardless of what he is saying? And will you have the firmness and courage to tell the truth? To practice goodwill harmlessness as a spiritual being you may have to say what the other person does not want to hear—but you must, otherwise you would be in conflict with the principle of goodwill and you could actually create harm if you placated him by agreeing with his perception.

But what happens when you find yourself facing a financial problem, a physical ailment or the loss of a job? You must talk to your lower nature the same way you would talk to anyone else seeking help and denying the Truth of Being. And the first thing you do is zip the mouth of your personality. You must etch in your mind the idea that only by *living* your good will you receive your good—and you cannot *live* abundance, wholeness and true place if you talk constantly about appearances.

While maintaining your poise as an observer and leaning on the spiritual understanding of the Divine Self, you speak to the lower nature. You view everything from the standpoint of Truth, and the Truth is that you are incredibly wealthy, wonderfully whole, and never "out" of work. The *I* of you is the Infinite All and is eternally radiating this Infinity of Good through you, but remember, for it to be expressed in visible form and experience, it first becomes *you*. So you transfer your personal identification from the little self who can do nothing to the Magnificent Master within who is doing everything now—to the Christ Self who embodies all the supply, wholeness and service there is.

You must remember that you are whole and complete right now. Your Universal Fullness is not something to come; it already is, and that is the absolute Truth that you must *live*. To deny that Truth by playing the misery-loves-company game, or by compromising your spiritual integrity just to please others and be nice and be loved, or by not living *with enthusiasm* the qualities of the Master Self, is to give the Law a fake I.D.—and for this violation you will be arrested.

Your consciousness, which is your life, will be confined to the limits of your false identification through the Law of Attraction, which will bring into your experience all those "human" problems with which you have personally identified. As we have said before, the Kingdom is finished, and for it to become manifest in Earth as it is in Heaven, it must not only come through you but *as* you. The *as* is the key word because it directly corresponds to your livingness, which is another way of saying that if you do not *live* love, *live* health, *live* abundance, *live* joyful relationships, you will not have those experiences on a permanent basis.

How do we live the Truth of our Being? To live (the verb) means to be alive, to have being, to be! It is being spirited, animated, eager, enthusiastic, buoyant, active, vigorous, alert.

Take health as an example. To *be* health you must totally identify with the Wholeness you already are. You stop paying so much attention to the physical body and you take the idea of Absolute Well-Being and become it. You ''soak'' yourself with the Idea from top to bottom, inside and out, day in and day out. You let the dynamic energy of Wholeness saturate your mind and animate your feeling nature, and you continuously live and move and have your being in this invigorating and nourishing Force Field of radiant perfection. You breathe only wellness; you think only perfect health; you feel only hardihood; you speak only words of completeness. You *live* health...you *live* your natural state of being eagerly, enthusiastically, vigorously. You stay poised and confident, detached from all appearances of sickness and disease in the world, keeping your mind in tune with the spiritual understanding of Absolute Wholeness radiating from your Perfect Self.

You do not commensurate with anyone regarding illness, for you never recognize anything but perfection in another. If a member of your family becomes ill, you do whatever is necessary to lovingly serve as a healing agent—spiritually and on every other level that is necessary. But you continue to be divinely indifferent, lovingly detached, and totally SELF conscious—standing firm in your Truth and speaking words that reflect only the Truth. You practice harmlessness for you *and* the other person by working totally in the Light of Truth.

The same process holds true for abundance, right relations and true place. Rather than trying to program the subconscious with mental treatments you *live* what you are. To live abundance you live *as* abundance. To *be* abundance you take on the rightful Identity *of* abundance. Incredible wealth is yours right now for use in the service of humanity's awakening, but it must become *you* before it becomes visible because your consciousness is the attracting agent.

To break the mold of insufficiency you may have to take firm and drastic action to shake up the lower nature as never before. Reason: you are changing identities at the root of your consciousness, and it may have to be a knock down and drag out battle to secure a permanent victory. If concern about finances occupy even a fraction of your waking hours, try this technique:

After a period of quiet meditation to get yourself centered in the Higher Vibration, begin to stir up feelings of strength, power, firmness and mastery. Then tell your personality-self that beginning that very moment you will no longer tolerate insufficiency, shortages, lack or limitation—that you have had enough of those games now and forever. Remind yourself who You are—an heir to the Kingdom of Lavish Abundance, the very Abundance of the Universe individualized as You, eternal Wealth in radiant expression. With great intensity make your point, make your vow, make your commitment.

You have now set the stage in consciousness to begin living as Abundance, and until the vibration is complete and in a permanent holding pattern, you will live only the Identity of Abundance. Your Higher Self is now the Master of Abundance and your lower nature is the channel for Abundance. Self-awareness joins with Abundance-awareness, and the radiation from within is pure Abundance. You breathe Abundance, swallow Abundance, walk in Abundance, sleep in Abundance. Everything related to God is Abundance and everything related to you as God in expression is Abundance. You maintain your mind and feeling nature in the fullness of Abundance. You look behind all appearances and see only Abundance. You are poised in Abundance, divinely indifferent to anything unlike Abundance. Who are you? Your name is now Abundance, and you live that Identity with all the strength, power, firmness and mastery of your consciousness. Remember...you always experience the identity that you live.

Moving beyond humanhood means moving beyond duality. In *With Wings As Eagles* I listed the "pairs of experiences" that represented human consciousness, the goods and bads of life. But in the list pertaining to spiritual consciousness there were only single entries: harmony, protection, happiness, wholeness, love, all-sufficiency, joy, peace. As you continue *living* your spiritual Identity and *being* the attributes of the Master Self, one day someone will ask you your name and instantly all the parts of Divine Individualism will blend as one, and the words will flash in your mind: "I **AM** the Christ of God." And silently and powerfully you will acknowledge the other person as One and the Same.

This is happening daily all over the world in the greatest spiritual awakening in the history of humankind. The scales are tipping...the critical mass is approaching.

I Keep My Promises—A Meditation

Imagine that you are tuned to the divine frequency of your Christ Nature and you hear these words of assurance pouring forth from within. Would not your life be changed? Ponder the words carefully, for they are from the everlasting Teachings of the One.

Yes, I keep my promises. I even had my assurances put in writing in passages of the Bible and in other sacred works. This was my contract with you, which did not require your signature to go into effect, for my promises are Law. Your only responsibility is to acknowledge that I exist and to believe what I said. It is as simple as that.

I have said, as it is written, that I will bring all the good that I promised, and I have promised much. I have said that you can call upon me in the day of trouble and I will deliver you, and I emphasized my love for you by saying that even before you call I will answer.

I have said that you must not fear, for I am with you, that in my presence is fullness of joy. I have asked that you trust me with all your heart, and lean not on your own understanding. Do you see the significance of this? It is MY understanding that pierces the illusion, not yours. It is MY power that removes the difficulty, not yours. Trust me. Lean on me.

Until you transcend the ego you can do nothing but add to the insanity of the world. That statement should delight you rather than create despair, for it removes the burden from your shoulders. While you learn and grow and let your consciousness unfold, I will do the work for you, through you, as you. But I must have your total attention. This is what I meant when I said that by acknowledging me in all your ways I would direct your paths.

I have promised you strange and wonderful things, if only you would place your faith in me and not in the outer world. I have said that I go before you to level the mountains, to harmonize anything that may concern you, and that I would perform that which is yours to do. Could I make it any plainer?

I have promised you unlimited prosperity, and contrary to your belief, I have not imposed any conditions. I give freely to saint and sinner; it is your consciousness that imposes the limitations. But I have told you how to surmount this obstacle.

As it is written, you are told that as long as you seek me you are made to prosper. The seeking is the key, for you cannot fully focus on the outer world of limitations while searching for me and my Kingdom within.

You have also been told that the meek shall possess the land and delight themselves in abundant prosperity. Do you know what ''meek'' means? It comes from an ancient word depicting that which is unresistant, easily molded. Look again at what I said: Those who do not resist their good and who consent to have their consciousness molded by me shall possess the land and delight themselves in abundant prosperity.

As it is written, I have opened unto you my treasure, insuring that you always have an all-sufficieny in all things. And when I said to simply love me and you would have peace within your walls and prosperity within your palaces, I was giving you the secret of the Law of Attraction. To love me with all of your being is to draw forth my Kingdom into your consciousness, and the fullness of my abundance is made evident in your world.

I have promised you wholeness, saying, as it is written, that I am the Lord your healer, that I heal all your diseases, restore health to you, and heal your wounds. This is not to come. It is. In truth, you are healed now...you are whole.

To those who revere my name, the sun of righteousness shall rise with healing in its wings. Think on this and see the simple instructions. A single eye on the Holy Self within receives Light into consciousness, revealing the absence of disease and the already-present reality of wholeness. I am the Fountain of Healing Life. Will you not drink freely of me?

I have promised you protection. As it is written, when you pass through the waters I will be with you, and the rivers will not overflow you, and when you walk through fire you will not be burned. Even if a host of enemies should encamp against you, you will not fear, for I will hide you. Stay close to me and let my shield shine through your consciousness to form a ring-pass-not.

Is anything too hard for me? No. And who am I? I am You. Not the human you but the Spiritual You, the Master You, the one called a priest after the order of Melchizedek. One day soon you will awaken, and my Consciousness will be yours and nothing shall be impossible to you. He who comes to you then shall never hunger, and he who believes on you shall never thirst, and he who follows you shall not walk in darkness. For I will be You and You will be Me, eternally the one and only Reality.

I keep my promises.

CHAPTER 5

The Final and Ultimate Mystery

Several years ago my "old man" (who represents a phase of my Higher Self) appeared to me in a dream and gave me the greatest secret in the universe. He spoke six words very slowly, then added what would happen if I followed his instructions: "all limitations in your life will vanish."

Let's pause for a moment and think about that. LIMITATIONS—whether in time, finances, health, relationships, career, or any other area—would vanish, be dissolved, if I did what he said.

I thought about the dream on and off for most of the following day, but by the second day I was continuing on about my business, trying to demonstrate prosperity, solve some personal problems, and figure how to sqeeze a 36-hour activity into 24.

I was reminded of the "secret" again years later and was told that it was the most misunderstood aspect of the Cosmos—that it is the final and ultimate mystery and the highest expression of alchemy. Still later the inner voice said that "it" is the Foundation Stone of the New Jerusalem. Yet, I continued looking for other secrets, formulas, techniques and processes, paying only lip service to this source of mystical fusion.

Time passed and I began to incorporate a part of the secret in my writings...even wrote a chapter about it in one of my books. But the full impact and meaning of this Master Link with God had not been totally embodied in my consciousness. While I had been given an advanced Cosmic Instruction years ago, I was teaching only elementary metaphysics in relating to this Divine Principle. At least that's how it appeared to me.

Then in November 1987, I was told in meditation that I could go no further in my spiritual growth—that I had moved from a human seeking the Light, to a human with an intellectual awareness of the Light, to a human with a subjective comprehension of the Light, but that I could not take the next intitiation in spiritual awakening until I was prepared to completely surrender my human sense of identity. This wasn't the "Final Mystery" but I think the admonition to renounce humanhood was Spirit's way of creating a vacuum to prepare a place for the laying of that Foundation Stone.

I thought at the time that I had surrendered my lower self to Spirit long ago—-that the detrimental aspects of ego were under control. With that thought I was quickly taken into the inner chamber to see the inventory still on the shelves. Oh my. I hadn't realized that I still had so many potential pulls, dormant reactions, lurking attachments and hidden judgements—all mixed up with a variety of false security blankets. They were all there, hiding in the dark, ready to spring into action if my vibrational level dropped to the point of vulnerability. And so a new cleansing process began.

From November 1987 through May 1988, Jan and I both had many powerful and highly significant dreams and meditative experiences. And in looking back we can see all the pieces fitting together into a picture that brought the "Mystery" and the "Secret" into greater focus. I won't go into all of those, but the bottom line was that we were given a new understanding of Creative Fire and how the New World of Harmony will be revealed.

As I have said before, we—you and I and everyone else who has chosen to do so—are here to save the world. No drama implied here. It is simply an assignment that we volunteered for eons ago. And the "saving" will be accomplished through a Power from the level of Spirit manifesting through the Soul and literally creating a new Reality on the third-dimensional plane. We are all agents for that Power, and once we have embodied it in its fullness, our will, intention and purpose can be used as a mighty force to heal and harmonize our miscreations.

I am about to reveal this Foundation Stone of the New Jerusalem, and as I do, please do not sluff it off as something too obvious, or insufficiently soul-stirring, or not radical enough to fit the description previously used for this "highest expression." If you do, you will be following my example from years ago and you will delay your initiations into mastery just as I did. Remember that I was told that it was "the most misunderstood aspect of the Cosmos."

The Final and Ultimate Mystery is...LOVE. Not from the level of personality, but from the Soul plane. Before we probe the secrets of this Foundation Stone, let's look at what it's *not*. Love radiating from the Soul is not affection or sentiment—neither is it human emotion that seeks to please or possess, nor is it an impractical ideal or selfish indulgence to make one "feel good." No, the Love that will transform the world cannot even be grasped in its fullness by the lower nature. It is simply too deep, intense, extreme and profound for people living solely in third-dimensional mind and emotions. Humanhood must be surrendered before the Light of this awesome Force can enter consciousness—but since we have been processing through that false identity, perhaps we are ready to begin this vital initiation.

To properly describe this "overcomer of every limitation" we must remember that there is only one Universal, Infinite and Eternal Energy, and that is the Energy of Love. It is the Energy that is the Cause behind all manifestation, the Power behind all creation—whether universes, solar systems, physical bodies, or the visible supply that we call money.

Love is the Divine Activity that impels and guides the

Laws of Evolution, Radiation, Attraction, Synthesis, Correspondence, and Transmutation. It is the Spiritual Vibration that carries the Divine Thoughtforms from Mind into concrete expression. It is the Cosmic Fire that manipulates time, changes matter, creates new form, vivifies all things, dissolves earthly karma, and emits a fiery auric radiation that lifts up the consciousness of all in proximity to its motivating power.

Love in its highest aspect is the Force behind the Will of God, the Vision of Christ, and the Action of the Holy Spirit. It is the Alchemy that will transmute the consciousness of nations and individuals, bringing all aspects of planetary life up to the Divine Standard of Spiritual Wholeness.

The Permanent Atom of Universal Love

That which we call an "individual" is in reality an energy field composed of storage cells called atoms. With every incarnation new atoms replace the old as karmic patterns are transmuted, however, one of the Permanent Atoms within each individual's energy field is the Atom representing the centralized force of Universal Love.

Einstein's Theory of Relativity tells us that an extremely small amount of mass can be changed into a large amount of energy. The "mass" referred to is matter—not "unreal" or an illusion in mortal mind, but the smallest particle of reality found on the physical plane, the atom. The word "matter" can also be traced back to its root word of *substance*, which is the essential quality of the magnetic field of the universe.

My point is that each one of us in an energy field of atomic substance, and the power of the universe is concentrated right where we are in the physical, material world. Within each individual atomic field is the Permanent Atom of Universal Love, the One that will trigger a self-sustaining chain reaction to produce a total transformation of the individual, and ultimately the entire collective consciousness. At the nucleus or central core of this Atom is the greatest concentration of energy in the world, and this energy is released through the fission (opening) of the nuclei.

The mechanism of fission within each individual is *an act of consciousness*. It is being consciously aware and recognizing that you have this Permanent Atom of Universal Love right within you now—followed by the understanding that it can be opened to release its awesome force simply by loving more intensely, powerfully and universally. Simple but not easy. The ancients said that universal love is difficult to apply to human conditions because of the selfishness of human nature. But we must begin somewhere if the sacred Atom is going to be split, and we start with love as we understand it at the present level of consciousness.

You begin where you are by pouring love into your immediate environment. With purpose of mind you remove unloving thoughts from your consciousness and practice *harmlessness* in thoughts and words. You keep loving in your small circle until you can expand your love nature and truthfully say that you love everyone without exception. And that includes everyone who has ever hurt you, anyone who has ever caused you mental suffering or emotional distress, anyone who has ever pushed your button and caused a flare of resentment. You must reach the point where you can radiate unconditional love to terrorists, murderers, rapists, child abusers, religious fanatics, political extremists, and any other so-called "evil" individual or group. You must be detached and loving toward all!

At the same time you continue to ponder, contemplate and meditate on this sacred Atom of Love within—seeing it magnified in your mind as a beautiful pearl, or a blazing jewel of light—and you love it with all of your being. You feel its presence in your heart, and with controlled visualization you see it slowly opening and see and feel its mighty radiation from its central core. Let that Love-Light shine through you and go before you to touch all souls, to open minds and soften hearts, to lift consciousness, and to heal, harmonize, prosper, protect, adjust, guide, strengthen, forgive. Practice love and loving daily as an initiate preparing for the role of Master of Love.

Then one day you will notice a decided shift in consciousness. Your love for all beings will have moved above human emotions, beyond conditional love, to an impersonal feeling of Will-for-Good for all universal life forms. And in a split-second the all consuming Fire will engulf you. Fission will have taken place and you become radioactive—literally. The chain reaction sets in and every atom of your being is transformed and you become a radiating Center of Universal Love.

As those Cosmic Rays flow out to touch the activities in your personal life, every aspect is healed and harmonized and you know that nothing can ever touch you again but love. And the power grows and the radiation moves through the lower kingdoms, all people, all nations—joining with other streams of Radiance until the Energy of Universal Love permeates and saturates Planet Earth and the world is restored to sanity.

Seven Days of Love...and continuing

Jan and I tried a seven day experiment in conjunction with the non-human program, and I want to share it with you. We made a commitment on a particular day to begin, with purpose of mind, to love as we had never loved before—and for seven days we vowed to *be* love, *live* love, and *radiate* love with all of the power and vibrancy of our beings.

We devoted our entire meditations to love and only love, and we worked with spiritual exercises to magnify the Love Atom and open it. We poured love into every situation that had the potential to pull on our consciousness, into every person we met or thought about, into all forms of life on this planet and beyond, and into the infinite reaches of the universe—all on an hour-by-hour, day-to-day basis.

On the third day I awoke hearing myself blessing with universal love the masculine and feminine energies throughout the infinite worlds, so it was obvious that a deeper level of consciousness had taken over even when I was asleep. By the fifth day the radiation was so intense that it was felt during most of my waking hours. I should also mention that during that week we experienced more peace, contentment and divine order than we can ever remember.

But there was more. Time seemed to work in our favor as we accomplished so much more in less time. Relationships with everyone took on a deeper meaning, visible supply moved to a higher level, guidance dreams were of greater frequency and clarity, and the vision of our purpose expanded considerably. Needless to say, the seven days of loving universally, vibrantly, intensely, and powerfully have continued. What a fantastic way to live!

Now let me go back to the beginning of this chapter, where I talked about the ''six words'' spoken to me by the old man in the dream years ago. They were..."If you would only love more." And then he added what would happen if I did..."all limitations in your life will vanish."

Love is truly the Final and Ultimate Mystery...the greatest secret in the universe.

A Meditation

Relax and let go. Be still in mind and emotions, and bring the focus of your attention to your heart center where the Permanent Atom of Universal Love is located. Say to yourself:

I am love, I am loved, I am loving. I feel the love vibration in my heart...I feel it expanding throughout my body. All there is is love...love...love...love.

In your mind's eye see that Atom of Universal Love in your heart center. Imagine it as a shining Crystal of Love, a glistening Jewel of Love. Contemplate it. Focus on the Love Diamond with clarity of vision, and know that all the love in the universe is concentrated right there, within you. Now in your imagination see it slowly open to release its light. See the radiant rays begin to flow, moving and filling your entire energy field...your mind, your feelings, your body. See yourself as a radiating Center of Divine Love. See the Love Essence radiating and filling the room where you are, and continuing to flow in streams of Golden Light...moving out across the land to encircle this planet. See the radiance of your Permanent Atom of Universal Love flowing like a mighty stream and see this world filled with the Light of Love. Now say to yourself:

I am Universal Love in radiant expression, and I now love as I have never loved before in my life. I silently, powerfully and intensely radiate my love, and I send it everywhere without exception. I see it flowing into my family, my loved ones. I see the Cosmic Rays of Love going before me to envelope and permeate everyone in my consciousness.

Those who have rejected me, who have hurt me, who have not recognized my true worth, I send my love to you with no conditions attached. I love you for Who and What you are. I love everyone without exception. I love everything without exception. I am the mighty power of God's love in radiant expression, and I let my love go before me to heal and harmonize every condition in my life.

Spirit of the Living God within, I am your love. I am your love in expression and I will keep this love vibration in my heart and thoughts of love in my mind, moment by moment, hour by hour, day by day, for I know that as I begin to love more and more, every limitation in my life will vanish and my personal world will become whole and joyous.

And the Light is growing and spreading. My Light of Love is joining with others who have opened the Crystal of Love and together we are saturating this world with love. The healing has begun, it is happening now, and I am doing my part to dissolve the limitations of humankind and restore this world to sanity.

I love as I have never loved before. I can love because I know Who and What I am. I am love, and I will never hold back my love. I will let it forever flow unconditionally, universally, divinely, powerfully, intensely.

I am love, and I rest now in the silence, thinking only of the love I am, and the love I give, and the love I receive.

All there is is love.

CHAPTER 6

Learning the New Song

From the moment you began reading this book you have moved, at least in some degree, from an ego-centered personality called "human" to a more spiritual state of consciousness—separating yourself from the third-dimensional belief system and opening to the Presence of the Master within. You have approached the first ring of the Kingdom Consciousness, and as you moved closer to center you felt the energy of the Kingdom radiating like mighty rays of the sun.

You are learning harmlessness by controlling your negative emotions while expressing your positive feelings. You are giving up judgement and are replacing human perception with spiritual understanding. And with this initial phase in the process of transmuting the human thoughtform, you have begun to love unconditionally—working with the Science of Universal Love as one taking an initiation to be a Master of Love.

You began the journey as if deep underground, and as you moved up toward the Light you may have been challenged by miscreations, monsters and demons. All of these deviants represent your own human thoughtforms, those created out of fear, guilt, hate, harmfulness, jealousy, resentment, condemnation, intolerance and bigotry. But knowing that you have to clean up your own mess, that no one is going to do it for you, you will face them all by accepting the unacceptable and powerfully acknowledging the Truth that ''I of myself can do nothing.''

In this paradox of human and divine, inaction and action, you may at first be unsure of yourself—and if you emphatically believe in one of the phantoms lurking in consciousness, it will quickly manifest in your life as a threatening beast on the path. But you will call it good, a blessing in disguise, for you know that false beliefs must be transmuted, either in consciousness or in manifest experience. And you will keep on moving ahead, casting other shadowy forms upon Spirit within with the attitude that those illusions ''are none of my business.''

At times the darkness may seem to overwhelm you, but you know in your heart that this is an initiation that every human on Earth must undergo at one time or another, and you will choose to do it now instead of later and get on with the business of cooperating with Spirit in the creative revelation of the New World.

An Awakened One who participated in the 60-day non-human program for evaluation has written that those who commit to the discipline of the program will enter into ''the Armageddon of the Soul''—an inner Armageddon corresponding to the Book of Revelation— which is necessary to insure the ''coming down of the New Jerusalem into our minds and spirits.'' I was also told that the Twelve tribes of the twelve thousand are here now, that each tribe must awaken to seal the door where evil dwells and bring forth the millennial reign of Christ in the hearts and minds of individuals, and that the identity transformation (the non-human program) is the paradigm, the archetype, of *those who will learn the new song.*

The ''new song'' was a reference to the 14th Chapter of Revelation (verses 1-3): ''Then I looked, and lo, on Mount Zion stood the Lamb, and with him a hundred and forty-four thousand who had his name and his Father's name written on their foreheads. And I heard a voice from heaven like the sound of many waters and like the sound of loud thunder; the voice I heard was like the sound of harpers playing on their harps, and they sing a new song before the throne and before the four living creatures and before the elders. No one could learn that song except the hundred and forty-four thousand who had been redeemed from the earth.''

Bible scholars have written that there are four main schemes of interpretations of the Book of Revelation, the fourth being ''spiritual'' without literal application. I feel that the book is indeed symbolic, but with definite coded messages for initiates. For example, the fourth verse of Chapter 14 reads: ''It is these (referring to the 144,000) who have not defiled themselves with women, for they are chaste; it is these who follow the Lamb wherever he goes; these have been redeemed from mankind as first fruits for God and the Lamb.''

In de-coding this transmission we see that 144,000 refers numerically to the final human initiation of completion (the numbers equal 9)—those who have gone through expansions in consciousness to reach the level of *spiritual understanding*. ''Not defiled themselves with women'' is a reference to the control of the emotional nature of the individual—those men and women who have transmuted the reactive emotions and are now living with purity of feelings and following the Christ within. These have recovered from the illusion of humanhood (''mankind'') and are the first of the awakened ones in the sevice of God and Christ.

By following the series of events throughout the book we see that the coming of Christ coincides with the end of the world. Yes! By realizing our spiritual identity (the Christ as I AM), the ''human world'' as we know it ceases to exist and we will see ''a new heaven and a new earth.'' From the opening of the scroll and the breaking of the first seal to the point where the new Jerusalem comes down out of heaven from God, the Awakening Process is described. And each one of us who is moving from humanhood to Christhood can certainly write his/her own Apocalypse, for the hidden miscreations must be revealed and transmuted if we are to stand on the mount in Christ and with the Father's name. But remember the underlying theme of this last book of the Bible. It is *Victory*. We shall be victorious...we will sing the New Song!

The Awakening of the Lost Race

By now I know that you have realized the purpose behind the non-human program. You have grasped the idea that by changing identities you change your consciousness from weakness to strength, from impotence to power, from subjugation to sovereignty. "I of myself can do nothing"—but *I as my Self* can do all things! We are not here to be pawns, victims or losers in a game called Life. We are not here as powerless little ants on some cosmic dirt clod. We are here to be Agents for Omnipotence, Distributors of the Creative Power of the Universe, Channels for the manifestation of the new Heaven on Earth.

Each one of us came into incarnation with an assignment and a purpose for being here. And we can complete that assignment and fulfill that purpose only by moving out of a sense of humanness and into the Four-Square vibration of Spiritual Consciousness. We cannot save our individual worlds and the world at large with fragmented minds and fearful emotions, but we can joyfully participate in revealing the Kingdom, the Power, and the Glory as the Divine Individuals—the Light Force—that we are in Truth.

As we continue to move beyond humanhood and incorporate more of the spiritual frequency in consciousness, our thoughts, visions, words and actions will be endued with new power. As the little ''i'' fades and the Master I takes command, the individual and group consciousness embodying the Christ Aspect will do its mighty work in dissolving the mortal sense in human circumstances. The Activity of Spirit will then take over human beliefs and reveal the Plan, Purpose and Dynamic Will in individual lives and on the world scene. While many will operate in a spiritual underground, others will receive assignments from within to go forth and be highly active and visible in transmutation work. But even in the latter cases it will not be "humans" who are given the marching orders. It will be Spiritual Consciousness acting in, through and *as* these men and women.

I have said that it may be presumptuous to call this non-human program "a Spiritual Philosophy for the New World," but it could be just that if we will *accept* the Idea of our Divinity and begin the process of transmuting the human thoughtform. Then, together, we can issue a call for a new Idealism and an unorganized religion based on Spiritual Realism. Together we can create a greater awareness of the spiritual revolution that is sweeping the world, and the effect it will have on the environment, the international monetary system, governments and political institutions, education, the judicial system, organized religion, and other areas of society. Together we can incite people to world service while living with passionate independence, magnifying the power of SELF-reliance while uniting their sovereignty in groups of like-minded Souls for the good of the planetary family. Together we can uncover and experiment with techniques and concepts of dominion and mastery and share the results. And together we can awaken to our true Identities and enter into the (re)construction stage in building the new Civilization. "And the Islands of Light will spread..."

The Lost Race. When Jan and I embarked on the adventure of seeking, finding and proving the existence of those whom we call "Superbeings", I had the thought that the entire evolutionary process could be greatly accelerated if only a certain set of "keys" could be found. Then later I realized that all of us are already evolved Beings and that the correct term should be the *Awakening Process*—and that the keys to the locks on the Dream Room door have been found. In fact, they were discovered thousands of years ago, but as humans we have ignored them, continuing to be sleep-walkers living the dream, enduring the Big Lie and experiencing the nightmare of hell and damnation. Why? Because some distant relative ate an apple from a private reserve? Come on!

The descent into third-dimensional materiality was a planned operation—a mission to experience our own creative expression. But we overdid it, and as the fog of miscreation set in, tens of thousands of Souls escaped. Others stayed behind and soon took on the vibrations of their miscreations, which shifted consciousness into a state of decline. Did you know that "sleep" and "slump" come from the same root word? Perhaps the best way for our ancestors to describe the sleep state was to call it The Fall. After all, "slump" is what we do when falling asleep sitting up.

It wasn't long before that first group of Light Bearers returned, descending upon the planet to help their brothers and sisters awaken. These were the spiritual "giants in the earth" as recorded in Genesis, but in time even these Beings "of renown" found their mastery slipping away through the misuse of their powers. (The third dimension can be a tough place to keep it all together.)

The end result was the destruction of their advanced civilization, and as I pointed out in *The Planetary Commission*, "...many fled to other parts of the world where their superior knowledge left a lasting effect. Evidence of their migration was seen in northern Spain, Egypt, Greece, Central and South America, and legends of all of these ancient civilizations refer to 'gods' who taught the secrets of the heavens and the earth."

Eventually, traces of these "giants" vanished and were later referred to in esoteric literature as "The Lost Race." Lost to recorded history, perhaps, but not to the unfolding mystery of the transmutation of the individual consciousness and the planetary ascension, which continues to be the work of the Light Force.

Are you one of them? We are told that more than a billion members of the Lost Race are now living on Earth, each resonating with the Truth of Being as strings in the Golden Cord. Are *you* a part of this Ancient Family? Now before you deny your Truth by thinking of all the ''stuff'' you are processing, let me remind you again that everyone has to get cleaned up after wallowing in the mud. Every disciple, initiate, adept and master who has come into physical incarnation has had to learn to dodge the slings and arrows of third-dimensional living, and some have certainly suffered by human standards and perceptions.

If you read the biographies of those who walked the Path to Cosmic Awakening and Masterhood, you will see that they did not have a bed of roses on this dense material plane. And the reason was because the race mind was continually nearing the danger zone—always teetering on the brink of going into a critical chain reaction. The almost shattering vibration of the Earth plane was a hindrance to even the most awakened ones and kept the memories sealed for most everyone else seeking the glory known in the beginning. That is not the case today, however.

There are more Souls on the Spiritual Path in physical form now than ever before, and the consciousness of each one of these men and women is literally changing the collective vibration and the world. The Light People may be completely unconscious of their influence upon the world. They may not even be aware of their power and radiating energy, but they are sufficiently open to permit an emanation of the impersonal Force of Spirit to act upon and soften the mass consciousness. And as the memory seals are removed through a commitment to *live* and *be* the spiritual life, the Power is personalized to raise each individual's life to the Divine Standard—and the *conscious* work of world service begins with great dedication.

Because of the massive outpouring of Light from above and on parallel lines from the awakening Souls, I believe that there are more opportunities now to achieve a level of mastery than at any time in recorded history. In Spiritual Arithmetic one plus One equals ONE, and when combined in group consciousness the Power of Transmutation is raised to the Infinite Degree. And that's why ten "giants" can save a city.

I said earlier that more than a billion members of the Lost Race were now in physical incarnation. This figure represents the first wave of Light Bearers who came in to initiate the Awakening and those who followed in support of the mission. Notice that I also said that they were "resonating with the Truth of Being." This does not mean that they have all realized their Christhood. Most have but a supportive vibration of Truth and are in agreement with the ancient teaching of Individual Divinity. But all of the seals are surely being removed, and one by one or together in groups, the lost Race is returning to Conscious Awakening.

Do you feel that your present status in life disqualifies you from being a member of this Ancient Family? It really makes no difference where you are, because some of the most advanced People began to lift the veil while serving as carpenters, unemployed poets, fishermen, peasants, students, school teachers, artists, writers, soldiers, men and women, all color of skin, educated and uneducated. I think you get the idea. "Rank" has no priviledges in the Awakening Process.

CHAPTER 7

What Are Your Intentions?

In the first chapter I stated our creed: *"Have nothing and you possess everything."* By surrendering all that you are and have to Spirit, the Master Self within begins to assume control and the personality becomes a channel for the Activity of Spirit. But do not even consider the possibility that you are going to spend the rest of your days in a sitting, listening, passive state of being absolved of all responsibility. Actually, your true work is just now beginning. Having moved (or in the process of moving) above selfish desires, fearful emotions and human reactions, you are reaching a state of consciousness based on Universal Love, and you are learning to be a radiating Center of that incredible Power. And as your consciousness takes on more and more of the Higher Vibration, you hear the words: "What are your intentions?" What is your answer?

If that question had been asked before you entered the cleansing, your answer would probably have reflected fearful emotions relating to unfulfilled personal desires, some purely selfish. Now, however, you can see with a higher vision and you are ready for acceptance in the inner ashram of the Master Self to share in the creative work.

In addition to an inner resolve to see wholeness in your individual world, you are moving toward a greater *group* orientation—more in tune with your spiritual family with greater focus on, and understanding of, the Universal Good that is the birthright of all. And so you are (or will be) ready to work with the Master within in fulfilling the law of Harmony and preparing the world for the Christ-ing of the collective consciousness.

You know that peace, prosperity, wholeness and harmony can only come to this world through individual beings—that individual consciousness is the inlet and outlet for the transmuting activity of Spirit. Therefore, you are now willing to accept the responsibility for being a vehicle for the Divine Expression. And the next step following (1) the surrender of the lower human nature, and (2) living as a radiating Center of Divine Love, is to (3) firmly establish you intention. Ageless Wisdom calls this "determining the motive and directing the currents"—and it is a vital step for all who consider themselves allied with the Forces of Light.

Looking at this third step, I ask you: What are your intentions? For some of you the answer may be an unemotional, detached yet loving urge to harmonize specific conditions in your individual world. Because you are processing through the Identity change and have reached a level of spiritual understanding, you are not fearfully reacting to the outer effect. You are poised and confident that it is the Divine Will that your life be filled with Light, but you recognize that a few dark spots remain due to an unconscious consent to certain race mind beliefs. Through firm *intentions* you will start to gather the power to transmute those patterns.

A number of you may have moved to an even higher perspective, and you feel that your intentions are more than just for your self or your immediate human family. Being more group conscious and more in tune with the needs of the entire planetary family, your intentions are to see their needs fulfilled. While this is a selfless, impersonal and loving action on behalf of others, you are not leaving yourself out of the picture, for an old esoteric law says: "To invoke the greatest good for others is to partake of the divine blessings for yourself."

Now let's look at a few intentions. We must each write our own from where we are in consciousness, but these examples can serve as starters. Also, as you write your intentions, ask yourself—"What is my *motive* behind this intention?" This will help you to establish clarity of purpose.

Intentions

My intention is to surrender all that I am and have to the Master Self within.

My intention is to become totally detached to the material sense of existence.

My intention is to be consciously aware of the Presence of God I AM and the Creative Activity of that Presence.

My intention is for all the activities of my life to be Spirit directed.

My intention is to serve Spirit and not my ego.

My intention is to practice harmlessness in every activity of my life.

My intention is to love unconditionally and radiate my love to all without exception.

My intention is to realize the Spirit of God within as my Source, Supply and Support.

My intention is to see all the people on Planet Earth living in a consciousness of life more abundant.

My intention is to see right relations among all the people on Earth.

My intention is to see the entire planetary family living in radiant health and wholeness.

My intention is for everyone on Earth to be in right livelihood, fulfilling the Divine Plan in loving service to others.

My intention is to do my part in transforming the collective consciousness and revealing the Kingdom of Heaven on Earth.

As you move into higher realms of consciousness your intentions will begin to reflect those of the Great Example, Jesus, and his instructions to his initiates—and you may feel from the depths of your being that ''I am to do the will of the One Who sent me, and to finish the work...to live as the light of the world, that all who come into the range of my consciousness shall have the light of life...to be the way, the truth, and the life...to know that all power is given unto me in heaven and in earth, and to go therefore and teach all nations, pouring into consciousness the cleansing power of the Word and teaching them to observe only the Law of Spirit which is Love and Will-for-Good.''

You say that such resolutions are beyond you, that they must be reserved for the messiahs of this world? Just who do you think you are? Regardless of the level of your present consciousness, the fact remains that the Reality of you, your Cosmic I AM Identity, was the One Who spoke from the Burning Bush, saved Daniel in the Lion's den, divided the Red Sea, multiplied the widow's oil, walked on water, raised the dead, cast out demons, blasted the fig tree, fed five thousand, made the blind to see, cleansed the lepers, healed the sick, and turned water into wine. In your True Nature you are God being You, the one Presence and Power Individualized *as* You.

Moses, Elijah, and Elisha did nothing that you cannot do, and Jesus said that you will do the works that he did— "and greater works than these" will you do—emphasizing the truth that "*nothing shall be impossible to you.*" When you consider the awesome majesty of your True Being, you begin to understand that problems, needs and desires are nothing but figments of your human imagination. Should not one intention be to rise above this false judging of appearances? Isn't it time to look within and recognize that your Divine Consciousness, which is the very Kingdom of God, has absolutely no limitations? If everything is complete and whole in your Supermind, which it is, then what are Its intentions? One is to control the personality and harmonize the conditions in your immediate environment. Another is the unification of the Self and the "not-self" resulting in the disappearance of duality. And the ultimate is the emergence out of the human kingdom to function freely in the Kingdom of God.

During the process of these initiations (expansions in consciousness) the Holy Self will help you stabilize the emotions, control the mind, awaken your spiritual intuition, and orient you toward the spiritual life and world service to fulfill your mission on Earth. Eventually your Divine Nature will be all that you have or know, and you will pass on under the Law of Ascension to higher work as part of the Divine Plan for this solar system. I bring out these points as a way of stimulating the development of your firm intentions, to show you that even in the establishing of spiritual goals there should be no limiting of your vision.

What you see you shall become. As Carlyle stated it, "*Have a purpose in life, and having it, throw into your work such strength of mind and muscle as God has given you.*"

Knowing that intentions channel energy into expression, work with formulating your own until you are sure that your motives are right and that the intentions are divinely inspired. Keep in mind that once you formally and firmly establish your intentions in writing, Spirit will work with you and through you to manifest them in Divine Order—through specific guidance regarding action you are to take, and through positioning to assure you that you are in the right place at the right time to receive and express your good. It is also valuable to review your intentions several times a day—memorizing them and calling them to mind often—to deeply etch the patterns in consciousness.

For many readers of this book, surrendering your humanhood, loving universally, establishing your intentions, and resting in the Presence to *let* the Master Self express through consciousness are the steps you will use in cooperating with Spirit to "make all things new." For the majority, however, that two-edged sword called "free will" may be preventing the maximum flow-through of the divine energies of adjustment. You may have willed so strongly and improperly through selfish desires that your consciousness is opaque in certain areas. In such cases additional work may be necessary—to include the power of will, controlled visualization, and a specific act of gratitude. This would mean that our "Spiritual Philosophy" incorporates seven specific activities to help us replace the human idea with the Idea of our True and Divine Identity. Let's look at those seven steps now in some detail—particularly the Will aspect.

The Seven Steps of the Non-Human Program

1. The first step is the surrender of humanhood, breaking the connection with our identity as humans. In essence, we give up our mortal sense of existence by acknowledging that "I of myself can do nothing." We become impersonal and detached to the mental-emotional drain of the material world and focus intently on the Spiritual presence within, seeking only a greater awareness of the Master Self and a deeper recognition of the Activity of that Self. We get the lower nature out of the way and let Spirit manifest the Kingdom through us. This first step also includes the practice of harmlessness and being emotionally detached from the "effects" of this

world. It means living as a Divine Individual with poise, power and spiritual Self-awareness.

2. The second step is to love as we have never loved before, unconditionally and universally, without exception. We may not love the personality, but we can love the Essence, the Truth, of everyone on this planet and beyond. We recognize the grand and glorious Love Crystal within, the Permanent Atom of Universal Love, and we magnify it through meditation, seeing it open and feeling its mighty radiation from its central core. And we let that Love-Light shine through us, and we continually live love, practice love, and radiate love with all the power and vibrancy of our beings.

3. As Spiritual Beings on the Universal Love Vibration, we are ready to cooperate with Spirit. Standing in an ocean of Love we now go forth to love and to serve according to our divinely inspired intentions. We look at our individual worlds, our spiritual family, and life on Planet Earth, and we intuitively know that which is ours to do. And so we establish our intentions, which become a part of our consciousness and serve as the patterns for the Divine Energies. We live with purpose in mind, and that purpose is made manifest in our lives for the good of all. And we stay alert to new assignments on the Path as a Divine Cooperator with the Master within.

4. Once our intentions are established we have the Divine Motivation to cooperate with Spirit. Now we must have correct understanding of the Will Aspect—the Will of God, and the use of that Will. Each individual has free will which means the free use of God's Will, for there is only one Energy of Will and that is the Will of God. In giving us the gift of Divine Will God transferred authority to the Spiritual Identity, the Christ, and this will-authority-dominion was then reflected in the personality or lower self where it became adulterated. This impure or ''watered down'' will was then used to create, which resulted in *mis*-creations. ''I of myself can do nothing'' is

just another way of saying that "I of myself can sure mess things up."

So we see that if we want the highest expression of Spirit in our personal worlds and universally, we must transfer our use of the Divine Will—we must relinquish it to Spirit. This return of Authority is accomplished through a command in the name of the Christ within, which shifts the power of will from the lower nature to the Higher Self and permits the Christ Energies to move through the Force Field *above* the level of the adulterated ego consciousness.

The Wisdom Teachings define will as "active intelligent purpose lovingly applied"—and say that by invoking the Christ Will, specific currents of energy are released to be expressed according to the formulated idea (intention) in the mind of the thinker.

To properly use the Christ Will we speak in a firm voice: "I surrender my use of God's Will and I invoke the Will and Authority of Christ." Now think carefully of your intentions and follow with this second invocation: "In the name and through the power of the living Christ within, I call forth the perfect manifestation of my intentions." You may then speak your intentions aloud if you so desire.

5. At this point, begin to formulate in your mind through controlled visualization the perfect scenes corresponding to the fulfillment of your intentions, seeing everything done, accomplished, finished, NOW! See this image of Divine Completion as a golden circle of Light, and once you feel joyfully confident that all the parts of the vision are in place, release the Thoughtform into the omnipresent Substance of the World Mother.

This release must be with an attitude of total *giving up*. You are planting a magnificent seed thought in Mother Substance, but if you do not let it go completely it will lose its potency. See the Thoughtform as a golden Light, and as you surrender it watch as it disappears on the screen of inner mind.

6. Now you are ready for a period of joyful thanksgiving and loving gratitude to the one Presence, the one Spirit, the one Cause within—the Divine Consciousness embodying the Will and Power of the Father, the Love and Wisdom of Christ, and the Creative Intelligence of Mother God, which is even now giving form and creating the experiences relating to your formulated idea.

7. The seventh step is to rest in the Presence, knowing that not only are your intentions being "made flesh" but the Universal Law of Harmony is being fulfilled through you by the Divine Will. You are now an Agent for God, a Distributor of the Divine Energies, and a Co-creator with Spirit—continually alert to new instructions and assignments as a participant in the Creative Process.

There are many ways to cooperate and create with Spirit. These steps represent ways that we have found to be most fruitful, and you are encouraged to experiment with them and judge for youself. Never forget that *consciousness* is the key and the door to the Kingdom, so in the final analysis it is what we do in our initiation work to cleanse, purify and expand consciousness that really counts. And the bottom line is...do we really care enough to want to change from the old human to a new creature in Christ?

What *are* your intentions?

CHAPTER 8

The Divine Stratagem

To be "four-squared" means that the individual is in balance—spiritually, mentally, emotionally, and physically. It denotes the whole person functioning in a Fourth Dimensional Consciousness and expressing the Truth of Being on the third dimensional plane.

This four-square symbolism can also be viewed from a cosmic perspective: (1) The Will of God, the Omnipresent Father, (2) the Love of Christ, the Universal Son, (3) the Intelligence of Spirit, the Holy Mother—all expressing as One in (4) the Person of Jesus Christ.

Where do you fit in this Holy Square? You are it! You are the Will of God, the Love of Christ, and the Intelligence of Spirit—and the story of the Divine Being whose birth we celebrate during the Christ Mass on December 25th is *your* story. Jesus' birth and life is a detailed map of the Path and a magnified vision of the Divine Stratagem, carefully planned to reveal to you your supreme value as an individual.

It has been almost 2,000 years since this Cosmic Proof incarnated on Earth as God's Perfect Example of you, of everyone, but collectively we did not believe God and we certainly did not believe this Divine Reflection of ourselves. Perhaps it was because his teachings were so twisted and distorted, his life so controversial, his truth so out-rageous. Or maybe our disbelief is simply a denial and disavowal of ourselves.

Jesus shattered the ring-pass-not of spiritual under-standing. He extended the frontier of Knowledge, thus providing us with an opening through which to move out of ignorance, fear, guilt and self-condemnation. But we retreated deeper into our "caves of darkness." Over the years a few "got it" and they would quietly and carefully leave messages at the doors of the caves for the ones with open minds. One by one they ventured out into the light.

Slowly the light spread and new secret societies were formed to explore the mysteries and prove the teachings. And in every case, in every place, Jesus was there...over-shadowing the group and radiating his Energy into the consciousness of the searching souls.

Meanwhile, in the depths of the caves the masses continued to huddle, watching the shadows and listen-ing to those seemingly with authority—those who thought that they could usurp the power of God. In ignorance they taught ignorance—and Jesus lovingly looked on, knowing that even in the human sense of time the lines of light and darkness would one day converge and the lower world would cease to exist.

Nothing can hold back the Will of God. No one can change the Divine Plan. Jesus came into this world to impress on the collective consciousness the Will of Reawakening and the Plan of Christing. This Cosmic Seed, this Divine Purpose, is part of our very being, and is the way out of the illusion.

The Message of the Records says, "You are the Holy One of God and all that the Father has is yours. You have simply forgotten, and in the forgetting you created a belief in a self that does not exist.

"I came to show you that you can remember and be born again in Spirit. I came to show you that through the symbolism of baptism you can, with purpose of mind and heart, let go of error by releasing all to the Spirit within.

"I came to show you the divine possibility of your perfection so that you will therefore be perfect even as your Father in heaven is perfect. I came to show you that once you have crossed out, crucified, the lower nature, you will be resurrected as the Divine Being you are.

"I came to reveal your Divinity by offering myself as an Example. I came to give you proof of your Identity."

What a glorious mission! But what do we do? We, unconsciously perhaps, continue to look at poor Jesus hanging on that old rugged cross as a symbol of suffering that we are supposed to endure while in physical form. How unhinged can we get? Yet we have chosen this idiocy and have interpreted it as a way of life.

Isn't it time to take Jesus down from the cross? Isn't it time to look again at *The Book of the Way* that he left for us and start following his instructions? Isn't it time for each one of us to claim the seamless robe and accept our inheritance as Beings of Light? So many millions have already done so and are following this love-being, joy-filled, fun-loving, peace-giving, freedom-speaking Elder Brother right into Paradise on Earth.

We are all on that path, too, because everyone who reads these words has already passed through that first gate—the first initiation of becoming consciously aware of the indwelling Christ Presence. But we must not become complacent or we will be pulled right back through the gate into the never-never land of upside downness.

The original esoteric (hidden) meaning of Christmas was to ceremonialize and commemorate the Christ Idea and be born anew in the Spirit of Truth. To the Initiates it was a holy ceremony to remember the rebirth with a rededication to the Master Self, the Christ within. Was Jesus left out of the commemoration? Hardly. His birth provided the framework, backdrop, scenario, purpose and meaning of the ceremony—so it was both a celebration of gratitude for the Great Example and Wayshower, and an observance of that first door leading to mastery.

A Time for Rededication to the Christ Within

The New Testament was written for the social consciousness of the time, and for the spiritual consciousness
of all time—with instructions in both law and grace. The
former is the tradition of organized religion; the latter is
The Book of the Way incorporating the coded messages of
the Mysteries.

Let's take the Gospel of Matthew and interpret a few
of Jesus' teachings as he spoke from the Christ Presence
on how to live life lovingly, peacefully, joyfully, abundantly, and freely.

"God's will for you, which is perfect harmony, is the
Word of God, and God has spoken. Therefore, God's will
is the only power in your life and harmony reigns
supreme. If appearances say different, they are false and
exist only in your mind as miscreations.

"Miscreations come from serving your ego and bring
hopelessness and despair. Divine creations, which come
from serving God, bring joyfulness and happiness. You
cannot serve two masters. Choose this day whom you
will serve.

"It is now time for you to let go of everything that
makes you unhappy. As you turn within to me, carry all
your burdens with you. Search your heart and mind and
bring everything that has ever troubled you, past and
present, into the Light. Hold nothing back. Be honest
with me, for I judge not. Release all to me, being consciously aware of what you are surrendering...all situations of conflict, all conditions of fear, all feelings of guilt.
Bring them all to mind, then give them all to me.

"By surrendering all to me, you will reach the point of
possessing nothing—nothing that can bind you to error,
to the false, to the unreal. And it is at this point that you
will realize that you have everything, that you are so
whole and complete that nothing can be added.

"There are attitudes of mind that will keep you firm in
your resolve to let go of the lesser in exchange for the
greater. In your meekness, which means being nonresistant to the good of God, you are blessed beyond imagin-

ing. In your mercy, which is simply tolerance and forgiveness toward others, you will receive the kindness of the universe expressing to you from all.

"Do not worry about anything. You have already been given the Kingdom, which means there is no lack in your life. In striving 'to get', you are denying the Kingdom, denying that which you already have. Live in the constant attitude of *having*, which is knowing the Truth, and you will be free.

"You must become as a little child, as one who is innocent, guileless—knowing that of yourself you can do nothing, but knowing that with God, all things are possible. This understanding puts your faith and trust in God as Cause, and in this frame of mind nothing is impossible to you.

"And now I will tell you the reason for every problem you have ever had or ever will have. I have told you to judge not lest you be judged. To judge is to pass sentence on; it is to make a determination. You have determined that you are something less than the sacred, holy Light of the World that I said you were. I have also asked that you not deny me, otherwise I would deny you before the Father. Understand now what this means. To deny me is to deny the Truth of you, for I am the Christ as you are. There is only one beloved Son in whom the Father is well pleased, and that is the Universal Christ whom we all share as the single Identity. To deny me—your True Self— is to deny your Identity, and this disavowal creates a false image which is not recognized, thus denied, by the Father.

"When you say in thought, word and deed that you are not Who you are, you are removing yourself from the creative power of God and placing yourself under the authority of darkness, your imagined self image. Acknowledge Who you are and live that holy acknowledgement at every moment. There are not two of you, one human and one divine. *You* are the only I AM; there is no other, there never has been. Strengthen this Truth even more by recognizing everyone everywhere as your Self, as the Holy One of God, and treat all as the Christ.

"Through this constant acknowledgement of your Self, the one and only Self, and the recognition of your Self, the one and only Self, in others, every problem in your life will merge with the divine solution...and the angels will proclaim your Heaven on Earth."

The Single Eye and the Light at the End of the Tunnel

While we are still looking at the messages in Matthew, let's pause for a moment and focus on the "single eye" that Jesus refers to in Matthew 6:22. The coded instruction really means having one-pointed concentration on your Destination. It means establishing the Main Priority in your life, the Single Purpose, and not letting anyone or anything detract you from that Master Intention.

This will mean relaxing your hold, your fixation, on the old world and the old ways—even giving up the outworn ideas that you may have adopted as a "New Ager"—even dismissing some of the gods that you have called on to fix you and give you happiness. For example, are you still looking for Light in the bottom of a bottle, in a pill, in a past life, or in metaphysical magic—or from a discarnate, a channel, a guru, a space brother, a book, or a crystal? Are you running away from "the system" and playing the spiritual game as an escape from responsibility?

Are you worshipping a particular diet as a way of storming heaven's gates? Have you, in your spiritual quest, become so spiritually pride-full that judgement and criticism are outweighing unconditional love and acceptance? Are your "causes" throwing you out of alignment with the basic principles of goodwill and harmony toward *all*? And isn't it time to bring down the curtain on your third-dimensional role playing?

You have learned the lines of the victim, the martyr, the dependent, the different, the misfit, the impoverished, the sufferer, the taker, the misunderstood, the abused, the unemployed, the overworked, the disadvantaged, the lonely, the unfulfilled, the ailing, the karmatized, the hippie, the yuppie, the preppie, and the dopey. Will you not throw those old scripts away and learn the new roles as a Conscious Mind, a Divine Individual, a Being of Power and Purpose?

Are you so caught up in New Age "buzziness" that you have lost sight of your reason for being? Are you becoming so organization-oriented that you have forgotten your individual Soul? Has the structure become more important than service? Have you forgotten that you are here to give, contribute and serve for the benefit of the whole?

These questions are not just directed to you; I am asking myself the same ones, so let's take a moment and *think*. Reaching a heavenly state of consciousness is a do-it-yourself project, but if we get so caught up in the third-dimensional project and forget our Fourth Dimensional Objective we will be like an artist painting one picture over another and continuing until there is nothing on the canvas but an undistinguishable glob. And that is what some of us appear to be, created out of our own experiences of superimposing such a kaleidoscope of colors and images on our screen of life that life itself becomes distorted and fragmented.

If you agree, it is time to pull out a fresh new canvas and start painting our life story with greater simplicity— the time for each one of us to get very clear regarding our purpose, our reason, our intention, and our destination—the time to start looking through the Single Eye.

"If therefore thine eye be single, thy whole body shall be full of light." This statement is a "secret" message in that the Truth of it is glossed over and ignored by the masses of humanity.

First of all, the "body" reference in the statement can be traced to the original word meaning "nature"—i.e. "if your concentration is on spiritual Truth, your whole nature will be full of light." And what is your whole nature? It is *Consciousness*—the bodies of consciousness represented by the spiritual, mental, emotional and etheric combined, your whole Energy Field as an individualized (undivided) Conscious Being. So we see that a one-pointed focus on that which is true and real will purify consciousness and open it to receive more and more of the Greater Light, which leads ultimately to the Final Awakening.

If you are ready to put the Single Eye into practice in your daily life as part of the non-human program, here are a few suggestions that just may save you years of wasted effort.

1. Keep the One within in your conscious awareness and each day dedicate your life to the One with intensity. Devote little time to the side shows. The Main Event is the awakening to your True Identity and taking your place among the illumined of the world as part of the Light Force assembling for the salvation of this planet.

2. Seek changes in your outer world by changing your consciousness. Trying to manipulate people and situations is not co-creation and will only delay your journey. Co-creation is working under Divine Guidance with trust in your Self. Is God not trustworthy? Is the Presence within not worth your trust?

3. Do not look outside your Self for your good, your happiness, your fulfillment. It all flows from within out, which means that *All* is within you now. Find it within and you will never be without.

4. Information leading to awareness can come from the sharings of others on the path, but the Realized Truth that ''makes all things new'' (adjusts conditions in your world) can only be imparted by the Master Self within. Listen, read, and study—then follow this opening process with the infilling from within by pondering, contemplating and meditating—and you will surely have the Experience. It is as certain as the rising sun.

5. Do not give power to an effect, for to do so will give people, places, things and conditions power over you. That is servitude, not mastership.

6. Do not run from responsibility. Enhance your ability to respond to the needs of this world by being and serving *in* the world. The "system" will be changed from within. To escape removes you from the transforming action taking place at the center of the human scheme where your divine energies are needed.

7. The Universe will not tolerate freeloaders disguised as spiritual aspirants. Find that which is yours to do in selfless service and do it to the best of your ability.

8. What you eat or do not eat will not make you more spiritual. Each individual has different bodily requirements based on his/her ray types, phase of life, and vibratory rates. Eat wholesome food but pay less attention to your physical body and more to disciplining your *emotional* body. Your physical system will then respond with greater healthiness.

9. Mind your own business, which does not include the business of what others are doing or saying. Your "spirituality" does not give you the right to force your opinions on anyone else. Criticize not. Judge not. Practice harmlessness even in your causes.

10. You create your own experience from the roles you play in life. You do have a choice. Choose now to change your identity from a suffering put-upon human to a Conscious Divine Being. Remove thyself from thy pity-pot and assume the Throne of Dominion as a Spirit-infused Individual of Life, Love, Light, Power, and Purpose.

11. If you have built an exclusive "New Age" fence around you, you may find that you are subjectively separating yourself from the planetary family. Remove all labels and barricades and see yourself in oneness with all life on every plane, in every dimension.

12. If you consider yourself as a part of a fringe group you will forever remain on the fringe. There is a main stream on Planet Earth called Life, and that is where you will find your greatest opportunity for service.

13. Place less emphasis on organizational structure and more on expanding individual and group consciousness. The organization is only as good, effective, or lasting as the consciousness that supports it.

14. Your Reason for Being is to process through a succession of expansions in consciousness until you arrive at the state of Perfected Being and awaken fully to your Divinity.

15. With every degree of illumination achieved your field of influence is extended. You become a radiating center of Light for the good of the whole, and sensing the needs of the world you mobilize all your resources to bring about the greatest amount of good to the greatest number of awakening souls.

Times are changing. Dynamic energies are coming down, vibrations are speeding up, and we are all moving toward the Greater Light. The evolutionary process for us as individuals and for the world is in direct proportion to our unfolding of consciousness, to our reawakening. Through the Single Eye we can leave the dream state, and the faster we do the more rapid will be the positive changes in the outer world.

We cannot hold back the transformation, and my guidance has been to "hold on to your hat." We are all quickly moving toward that Light at the end of the tunnel, and this time it is not a train.

CHAPTER 9

I Already Know That

A few years ago Jan and I found ourselves (symbolically speaking) standing before a door that seemed to be locked. To find the key we began a dedicated and disciplined program of going apart from this world and entering into a meditative communion with the Master Self within for a total renewal of consciousness. This revitalized intensity lasted more than two weeks, and each day we shared with one another any new revelations that had come through.

On Day One I excitedly told her about a "New Truth" that I had received. She looked at me for a moment and then showed me some early notes on the non-human program where I had already written what I now thought was a new revelation. On Day Two she shared something that I considered very profound, and when I said "we're getting close" she replied, "It was here all the time in one of the chapters in *The Planetary Commission*."

Almost every day we discovered what we considered "the answer" in something that one of us had already written. Finally on Day Twelve, she said: "You know, we have both received a lot of divine inspiration over the years, much spiritual knowledge, but if we just share it with others and forget about it, we haven't been true to Spirit. We were given the lessons to master, truths to realize, which we shared in the books, but then we went looking for something new and more profound. I think we had better start practicing what we are teaching or we're going to find other doors closed to us.''

Guess what? We began anew to convert spiritual understanding into realization by embodying in consciousness the truths we had written about—starting with the original notes on the non-human program. We called it our Journey of Re-remembering.

During one of the Quartus Gatherings on The Guadalupe River Ranch a woman asked my advice about a challenge she was facing, and when I gave her my answer she said, ''I already know that.'' The truth is, if she really *knew* that, the challenge would not have entered her life in the first place. So maybe it's time for us all to begin again as little children. Maybe it's time to bring some humility into our lives and admit that we do not have all the answers. And maybe it's time to start practicing the Truth that we so eagerly share with others so that we can be the Teachers of Wisdom that we were sent in to be.

The challenge that Jan and I faced dissolved because we went back to the state of mind that says ''I already know that'' and began right there to replace ego with Spirit. In essence, we returned to the principles of the non-human program and started over as if we knew nothing, and in the process certain truths became *real*, which expressed as keys to open doors. Each one of us must detach ourselves from the ego and move into a total reliance on Spirit. We must cut the cord on the human sense of being and let Spirit be in absolute control of our lives. Nothing is more important then this.

The reason for every challenge. Speaking of egos, I believe with all my heart that every challenge faced by any incarnate being can be traced directly to this insane part of our consciousness and the loony games it plays.

Every problem with health, finances, safety, career, relationships is all ego and its belief in separation and illusions. No wonder that "Course 102" in the Mystery Schools was to destroy the ego. They knew of course that the ego was in truth only an illusion, so the "destruction" was to reverse the trend of mind away from the lowest aspect and to surrender everything to the Highest.

The students did not attack the ego with the idea of killing it. They let it die by attrition, by refusing to acknowledge that it exists. The Masters did not teach the students that they were both human and divine, that they lived on earth and in heaven too, that they had to take the good with the bad, that they had to evolve out of imperfection into perfection, or that ego and Spirit were co-creators. There isn't a hint of this kind of deception. The whole focus of the teachings was that each individual is a Divine Being *already* possessing the Gift of the Kingdom and eternally living in the Heavenly State, that bad and evil were make-believe, that everyone was already perfect, and that Spirit creates only through a Mind in alignment with Itself. What part does the ego play? It doesn't. It was left out of the script completely.

Why does it take us so long to "get it"? Why do we content ourselves with anything less than perfection? Right at this moment we have everything we could possibly desire for all eternity—we have it all and we have it now. This is God-Truth! But what do we do? We run around playing "as if" this were not true. We put the emphasis on the getting, the fixing, the manipulating, the scheming, the protecting, the justifying, and on the fearing. It is a good thing that Spirit has infinite Love and Patience.

Moving past the ego to establish right relations. From the letters that we have received over the years, it seems that the primary challenge among my readers is relationships—particularly with that "certain" man or woman. Let's zero in on this for a moment and see if we can move past the ego mind-set of "I already know that."

At a conference of the International New Thought

Alliance, Jan delivered an address entitled "There Is Only One Relationship." The bottom line was that the closer the relationship you have with your Master Self within, the faster the "ideal one" (along with all right relations) will be drawn into your life. Oh yes, you already know that. Alright. Let's look at it from another angle.

Consider your entire world simply as a screen onto which you are projecting that which is your consciousness. In the area of relationships, what you are seeing in others and receiving from others is a projection of what is inside of you. These are mostly unconscious thoughts and feelings, those that have been repressed. But all energy must be expressed in some way, and repressed energy is expressed through projection, i.e. putting it on someone else so that you can experience certain characteristics of yourself in another person and learn from the experience.

To be specific, if you say that "no one wants to make a commitment anymore," you are really saying that *you* don't want to commit yourself. And perhaps this is because you do not feel worthy—you are not worth being committed to. The root of this unworthiness could very well be some form of guilt lurking in the depths of your consciousness, a guilt for past wrongs on which *you* have condemned yourself and therefore have to be punished. What you are projecting is "Don't get too close and don't appear interested in me because I have sentenced myself to a life of separation from a loving relationship." The other person picks this up and plays it out for you, and all the time you "thought" you were seeing yourself playing the role of an interested, warm, loving, cheerful, witty, fun-to-be-with person. So when the rejection comes you are totally mystified.

In *Practical Spirituality* I wrote that "Everyone in your life is there by the Law of Attraction. And whether you consider them good, bad or indifferent, they are there to help you experience your self." (And) "If you feel a negative emotion about a personality characteristic in another person, chances are you have that same flaw in your consciousness, otherwise you could not see it in others.''

What I am saying in the above quotations is that everyone in your personal world will give you the opportunity to experience your self through projection, which can work in two ways: (1) Someone to whom you are attracted may reject you based on a radiation of distorted ego energy from the unconscious level of your mind, which either turns them off or enables them to play out your unconscious feeling for you. This rejection is a signal that you are being sabotaged by something within *you*, having nothing at all to do with the other person. And (2) someone can act as a mirror for you, enabling you to consciously see, sometimes in great detail, exactly what ego characteristics you are projecting. Remember, it is never ''out there''—it is always within.

Making all things new. To enjoy right relations with all people we must know our adversary. In the Wisdom Teachings the ego is called ''the Dweller on the Threshold''—and is described as the sum total of the evil desires, past mistakes and weaknesses, all perverse motives, and the personality defects of the lower nature. It is a vitalized thoughtform representing the principle of duality including wrong mental attitude and every controlling fault in consciousness.

Once we know what we are dealing with we can begin the process of transmuting this destructive energy through the Law of Substitution—in other words replacing the lower with the Higher, which is the primary objective of the non-human program. And one of the most effective transmutation activities is found in the words recorded in Revelation 21:5, as the Christ says *''Behold, I make all things new..''* From this statement we find a coded message of salvation.

Christ in you, the Master *I* of your being, makes all things new. This tells us Who does the creative work— not ego but Spirit.

Christ, the I THAT I AM, *makes* all things new. This is the Activity of God which creates, builds, produces, forms, causes, delivers. It is the Spirit of God in action through you—not in the future but in the NOW!

Christ, your Divine Identity, makes *all things* new. No qualifications here, nothing left out. Your entire world is changed from ego madness to reflect the Heaven it is in Truth.

Christ, the Spirit of You, makes all things *new*. Omnipotence in continuous unceasing thrusts of Divine Energy completely restores, renews, regenerates and rebuilds your life and world according to the Divine Reality. All of this is happening at every moment in time, but remember, Spirit can do *for* you only what It can do *through* you. And any obstructions, blocks, impediments and interferences are caused by the Dweller and the insanity that this thoughtform represents.

How do you clear the channels? Through an activity that impairs the dweller more than any other. It is called *surrender*, not to the mad hatter on the threshold, but to Spirit. It is a *giving up*—a casting upon the Holy Fire within all the aspects of your mental-emotional system that it feeds on, and this must be done daily.

Every single day, and hour-by-hour if necessary, until you are safely and permanently in the Secret Place, you must release everything that has caused you fear, anger, guilt, hurt and depression. These can almost always be traced to your wrong thoughts, wrong words, and wrong actions. Recall the cause. Recapture the situation and bring the whole scenario into the Presence within as if on a rolled up canvas and cast it upon the Holy Fire. It is a law of the Universe that whatever you surrender to Spirit is always purified, thus unblocking Spirit's avenues of expression through consciousness.

Rather than affirm your way out of a situation, why not simply give it up? Do not suppress it with a mask and drive it underground as food for the Dweller. Release it to Spirit within and let the never failing Law of Adjustment set you free. Hear the words again from the Magnificent I AM that you are: *"Behold, I make all things new."*

The Answer, regardless of the question or the problem, is always the same. The Holy One within, your Master Self, is the Answer. The desire for a meaningful relationship is a desire for oneness, a desire for something that you already have, and your Spirit is expressing now to reveal its reality. But do not suppress the desire, the need, or the feelings that tell you that there is emptiness in your life. Bring them all to the surface and look at them. Look at the loneliness, the frustration, the fear, the sadness, the anger, and the guilt. Expose all of this darkness of ego to the Light of Spirit, and then admit that you made a mistake, the mistake of letting your ego control you. Remind yourself that your ego can do *nothing*, which is the creed that we agreed on as the first step in the non-human program. And the follow-up statement was "Have nothing and you possess everything."

Think what this means. "Having nothing" means that you have taken all of the ego's insanities regarding relationships and have willingly given them all to Spirit within, a total surrendering to where nothing is left of the old repressed energy. And at that point you "possess everything" for your holy Self in now in control, replacing the ego's illusions with spiritual reality. What is this reality? Nothing less than the perfect complement to your soul. And as you stay in that spiritual vibration, *all* relationships are healed. As Jan has said so many times in her lectures, "there will be so much love in your life that all you can do is give it away." You know what happens then.

But you do not stop with a new reality only in relationships. You make the whole circle complete. You remove your finances, your health, your creative expression, and everything else in your life from ego influence, commit to Spirit, decide for Christ, choose the Holy One, and start living the perfect life that you were meant to live.

Ego gives you anger, despair, fear, and guilt. Spirit gives you love, joy, peace, and freedom.

The choice is yours.

CHAPTER 10

Escape from Darkness

If you had been in prison for most of your life and suddenly discovered a means to escape, the idea of freedom would be thrilling—yet you would anticipate that certain risks would be involved in making a safe getaway. The same premise holds true in your deliverance from the bondage of humanhood. As you make a firm and definite commitment to spiritualize the lower nature, all of the old negative thoughtforms and error patterns will rise to the surface to be transmuted. Everything that you have not cut the cord on will start pulling and jerking on your emotions, and all of the savage instincts of your nature will be called up—in truth to be tamed, but from their perspective, to control.

This is necessary if you are going to live in and as the Kingdom Consciousness. As I have said, the Master Self within thinks, sees, and knows only perfection and harmony, and these Divine Thoughtforms are carried in waves of Creative Energy through individual consciousness. If the vibrations of the lower nature are not in accord with the flow, the result or effect will be less than the Divine Standard. That is free will in action, the individual's freedom to believe anything and to conjure up false images to divert the Divine Expression.

As humans we want one thing but think another and the result is a terribly mixed manifestation. We try to get around this as metaphysicians by controlling our thoughts and emotions, but we soon find that it is easier said than done—and we finally decide to let it all go. We let go of the rope and totally surrender to the Holy Self within, knowing that "I of myself can do nothing." We put our trust where it belongs and work daily for a deeper awareness, understanding and knowledge of the Presence within. And as the Light begins to radiate into the lower nature, all the "stuff" in the memory bank is exposed; all the fears, guilt, resentment, condemnation, and self-disgust are uncovered and revealed in their stark nakedness. Thank God! Now they can be dissolved, transmuted, replaced by the Love Patterns of the Living Christ.

This is truly an initiation that every "human" must go through to achieve mastery, and I know that the people who originally participated in this experiment as a test group have taken steps up the Mountain that will never have to be retraced again.

The early volunteers. In January 1988, I asked for volunteers among the members of the Quartus Society, the membership group of the Quartus Foundation. They were given the basic requirements for the non-human initiation and were asked to participate for a period of not less than 60 days, keeping a spiritual journal of thoughts, feelings, guidance, and actions—and to share with us any major changes that were experienced in the outer world. More than 500 men and women in several different countries joined in the test program—and most if not all found it to be the Divine Solution in rising above the trials and tribulations of humanhood.

In the ascension process, however, hardly a one escaped challenges. But in moving through these dimly-lit nights of the soul they found pronounced energy and vitality in their daily lives, a heightened sense of intuitive knowing, better control of emotions, new spiritual understanding, and greater joy and serenity. There was a deeper sense of dominion as Spirit used the improved vibration in consciousness as an outlet to solve old unresolved problems and meet current needs "in a timeframe never before experienced." Without exception everyone learned valuable spiritual lessons, and even the ones who "stepped in quicksand" in the early stages found the way out and broke through barriers that were previously considered immovable.

I am going to let a few of these pathfinders talk for themselves, and I ask that you carefully study these excerpts from their case histories. Each one is a teaching tool and a piece of the map showing the escape route out of the darkness.

Results of the 60-day Non-human Program

If your foundation becomes shaky, rededicate and recommit.

"I give total and complete credit and thanks to the non-human program for the recent receipt of monies. I just formally started the program about ten days ago and incredible things have already begun to happen. It seemed to take about three days for me to start becoming aware of an expanded consciousness 'at work'. Though I've been a dedicated believer and doer for years, there was something quite dramatic that occurred when I surrendered ego—*really and formally surrendered* upon beginning this program.

"Initially I felt exhilarated and greatly relieved of the 'impossible' responsibilities and was very aware that THIS was where the Christ within had been trying to lead me for a very long time. Immediately I was guided to take corrective measures for previous projects and was given a new idea for quickly turning my finances around. I began the new project being more aware than usual of some very special and constant Guidance and 'Doingness' in and through me. A friend was staying with me and the project is to benefit her also. We were both so delighted and thrilled to note that time after time for the next five days it was clear to both of us that I was actually the vessel through which this idea was being produced. Everything went in place so smoothly, so beautifully, and with a degree of skill that really astonished me.

"Then came the day of the sale. Sometime during the previous evening and certainly as I prepared for the sale that morning, my ego slipped in and took over again. Some last minute Guidances were ignored, others were 'put on the shelf for next time', and somewhere along the line I became very attached again to all that was going on—and to all that I had so recently let go of.

"The sale flopped on its face. My friend and I were left feeling stunned. Yet (and this is why it's so important to be surrounded with friends of like mind), we both knew that right up to the day of the sale I was being spiritually led from the inception of the idea itself right on through its production. I reaffirm this because by the end of the day I was having serious doubts about my ability to recognize spiritual guidance. As a personal witness of all that had occurred, my friend was able to be supportive as I regrouped myself.

"A meditation shortly after the sale didn't reveal any particular information. I went to bed feeling devastated and greatly confused. The next morning the answer floated to my waking consciousness bright and clear. It went something like this: 'You let Me develop the idea and work through you to put it together, then *you* took over and tried to sell it with all the frills and flashes of the mortal mind. Didn't you know that it didn't need all that? If you had let Me finish My job, you wouldn't have had nearly the work to do that you did (the day of the sale) and the product would have sold out'.

"I immediately did another prayer and meditation of recommitment and promised to be more diligent about being a silent witness. The next day a check came in unexpectedly (right at the 11th-and-a-half-hour) without which some very urgent needs would not have been met.

And, per yesterday's guidance, I am spending this week reworking the project to include those ideas that I had previously set aside.

"This Dawning has brought such relief, brightly ablaze with new faith, confidence and Knowingness of Who and What I am."

In following the escape route we must be constantly aware of our reactions.

"The 60-day program was an eye-opener. Whether it is a pig pen or a spider's web one gets trapped by their own consciousness. Needless to say I got caught many a time during the day which proves that I needed to pray without ceasing. When my thoughts were earthly or human, I got caught. Every step, every second, I needed to be consciously aware of my reactions. I needed to give up the thoughts and feelings of the lower self because I was tested constantly. I needed to trust my spiritual consciousness like those astronauts needed to trust no gravity when they took their first step in outer space."

Freedom is being willing to experience anything without judgement.

"The non-human program has officially ended. What a tricky way of totally changing people's lives! I knew when I began that it really would never end, but that was too scary—two months I could handle. First of all, knowing that there were others participating with me was a great feeling. Having the support, the consciousness and the lightness of it being an experiment were perfect.

"I went through many phases of growth, learning, cognitions, releasings, healing—all rather rapidly. This, of course, is still happening. All of my fears, beliefs, desires, anxieties, anger, lacks, limitations, etc. came blaring up and hit me right in the face. I was very shocked and very overwhelmed at first, knowing that there was much-too-much human crap to keep my mind focused on Spirit. I felt such despair yet I kept on with the program every day.

"I am now in a very different consciousness than when I started a mere two and a half months ago. In one shift of consciousness I even gave up the desire for freedom and enlightenment, knowing that what we believe, label, judge and compare is what we get, when all there is really is IS-NESS. Then in the next shift I became willing to experience all the 'bad things', unspiritual things, even resisting resistance. It became a fun game...a thought would come in like 'Oh, you are so self-indulgent', and I would say 'Great, I really am. I love it, I choose it, and I am going to totally experience self-indulgence'. And guess what? Poof, gone. I quit judging and resisting my thoughts and they either just lightened up or disappeared entirely.

"I've now learned that freedom is being willing to experience anything—without judgement. I knew all this stuff theoretically—now it's a part of my Beingness."

A knowing of oneness in the moment of forgiveness.

"The non-human program was a most interesting experiment and beautiful experience for me. In looking back over my spiritual journal I find these thoughts: The experiment is an experience required of every soul...sooner or later. Daniel in the lion's den knew this— giving energy to the appearances of the beasts he could crumble, but he turned to the invisible power that overcame the world. The real test is ever living with such OPENNESS to Spirit that Spirit lives in and through us. It's like a Secret Service of listening to and being with Spirit, which is our natural heritage. In practicing Spirit steering through appearances, something happens—like the scene melts and one becomes warm and full of love more real than appearances ever were. The forms are still different but through the formless, invisible essence of all things there is a bonding. In Einstein's relativity the atomic structure has no boundaries. As Schweitzer in Africa watched the muddy rhinos at sunset, he felt the

ONENESS—his 'reference for life'. Every man knows oneness in the moment of forgiveness.''

Live as the Whole rather than the part.

''During the 60-day period I noticed a synchronisity about the thoughts that I was receiving and how they corresponded to what was occurring in the outer world, not only with myself but with everyone around me. What bubbles up most is the awareness of knowing that part of myself that is spiritual and living as the *whole* instead of the part. This idea was the basis for all that I have learned on the spiritual path. In the past I have learned 'Truth' and with each truth came a clear understanding of the whole. The non-human program is the visible landscape of the picture. We have given the brush to the Greater Artist that he may create a Masterpiece, and this is the foundation from which the picture will form.

''There were also times when human consciousness seemed to outpicture itself more than ever before, and this thought brought me on track: 'As we journey up the Mountain we are releasing ALL of the attachments buried in consciousness. If we step on a loose rock, realize that the avalanche is behind us.' When I have committed to spiritual livingness I have left my humanness behind.

''On February 16, after the Mardi Gras celebration was over, I saw a priest (on TV) placing ash on a woman's forehead. He said, 'From dust you have come, to dust you shall return.' That triggered this thought: 'From dust *humanhood* has come, to dust it shall return.' Humanness is not lasting therefore not *Real*. I found this to be a powerful affirmation when burning (on paper) my human sense of being.

''On March 8, I experienced a feeling of everything around me moving in a forward direction—that's the only way I could explain it. I saw a film and each frame was an expression of my life, and the inner voice said, 'Spirit goes before you to light the way, but more so it is moving into manifestation through your consciousness of God.''

Look only to Spirit for all needed things.

"After beginning the 60-day program with my little Quartus group here in Germany, I was convinced that our efforts had somehow gone awry. But after reading about the experiences of others I realized that things happened just as they were supposed to. My neat little world was thrown so off-kilter that I thought I was truly losing my sanity at times. All my fabricated 'support systems' in the outer world collapsed under the weight of dependency that I had misplaced on them. My employment situation was drastically changed—in retrospect, for the best, naturally. My 'last resort' of always believing that my family would bail me out financially, should I ever need it, was dashed when my father lost his well-paying job and a large portion of his retirement fund at the age of 60. (He has since begun his own business, which he had always dreamed of doing.) Then my lovelife fell apart and all of this within a two week period.

"The only thing that kept me on track were my spiritual studies. Awakening in a cold sweat at 3 a.m. only prompted me to grab my spiritual notebook and meditate myself back to inner peace with the conviction that God was in charge and there was nothing to fear. I made it through this period of upheaval and awakening as did my friends who also embarked on this program.

"I expected smooth sailing, total inner peace and no conflicts when the 60-day program began. What I got was the biggest step I've made to date in that direction and my gratitude is boundless. Realizing that calling 'no man your father on earth' and looking only to Spirit for all needed things was the greatest lesson I could have learned."

My life is filled with the Light of God.

"After dedicating myself to the 60-day program of completely turning myself over to my higher Self, the Spirit of God that dwells within me, in my mind's eye my ego became a large angry octopus during a meditation. In order to put it away permanently it seemed like a good idea to stuff it in a box, then nail the box shut. Ego put up a terrible fight, but I finally nailed the box shut. Suddenly in a great thrust of energy he began to force the nails out and was once again struggling to free himself. So, in my mind, I put some steel bands around the box, fastened them securely, put the box in a nearby boat, rowed the boat far out into the ocean and dropped it over the side. That was that, or so I thought.

''The next evening my mind became a battlefield between ego and Self, positive and negative, good and evil, whatever you care to call it. For a few hours I felt as if I were being torn in two. My ego was screaming at me to forget all this stuff and be like a normal person...selfish, greedy, sick, full of hate. 'Forget all this God-within stuff; you are wrong to believe such things', on and on it went. For a few hours I feared for my sanity. Only after I listened with earphones on and the volume high to my favorite music did the clamor of the battle calm down.

''The next morning during meditation the thought came to me that I was not supposed to *destroy* my ego, only control it, so I went down to the beach (in my mind's eye) and there on the sand was the wooden box, badly battered, and the tentacles of octopus were outside, still struggling, covered with blood, but still struggling.

''In a very soft and kind tone of voice I spoke to it...'I am sorry for what I did to you, but you must realize that I must be in control of my life, not you. I am going to let you out of this box, but you must remember that I am in charge of you, not the other way around'. I unfastened the box, and suddenly ego was no longer an octopus, but a cute little puppy...black with brown spots. He wagged his tail and licked my hands as I stroked his head. I told him that he was good, that I loved him, but that he must be constrained. He didn't mind the leash when I put it on, nor did he mind the pen I put him in. Leaving him with an ample supply of food and water, I closed the pen gate and went back into my world.

''From time to time, in my mind, I checked on him and

he seemed content in the pen. He greeted me with a wagging tail each time I refilled his food and water containers. I was more and more aware that I was spirit, and that spirit seemed to be guiding me along in my life, but a few mornings later in meditation, when I checked on him, I was shocked to find that my 'him' ego had just given birth to three darling puppies. 'She' snarled, bared her teeth and growled at me as I approached. In fact, I feared going close to her. In my daily life I was once again having problems in releasing myself totally to my God spirit. As the mother dog snarled at me day by day, day by day my worldly self seemed to once again be in control.

"During a meditation one morning, the thought occurred to me that I was still trying to confine my ego instead of controlling it, so I went back to the pen time after time trying to make friends with the mother dog, Ego. The puppies were growing and frolicking around in the sunshine. Finally after several days she let me pet her once again, and I explained to her that perhaps I shouldn't have put her in the pen, that I had decided to let her out. When I opened the gate she bolted out and ran in wide circles, round and round, out through the nearby woods. Occasionally she would stop, roll over and over in the dirt, then get up and run in circles again. Finally she ran over and sat down beside me, exhausted, and once again she licked my hand as I petted her. I told her that as long as she was a good dog she could stay out of the pen, but that she must always behave. She responded when I commanded her to 'Sit' or 'Stay'. Needless to say, my life was immediately running smoothly again.

"Since then things have continued to run smoothly most of the time. The puppies are most obedient and so is the ego—most of the time. Usually she just lies in the sun on her back, half asleep. Whenever I look at the puppies they always 'Sit'—up on their hind legs with their little front paws limp in front.

"The thought occurred to me that the mother dog is the ego that has been with me throughout my life. She will eventually be around no longer. The new puppies are my chance to have an ego that is trained from puppyhood to do as I say, and not control my life. Mother dog ego seems to grow weaker as time moves along. She is still around, but is not a fighter anymore. She seems content to just lie in the sun. And my life is filled with the sun—the Light of God.''

All of life on every level is coming together for me now.

''On the rugged path to Mastery and Christhood, when I've stumbled and fallen, you have picked me up. When I cursed the darkness, you lit me a candle. And now, instead of handing me the fishes (as I have requested), you are teaching me how to fish so that hunger for full union with God and service to mankind are fulfilled. It has been 2 1/2 years of growth and evolution (not without tears and pain) on my spiritual quest and path. And now, the final studies and exams with the Non-Human Program. I hope to graduate to the summit soon. All of life on every level is coming together for me now.''

You do the accepting, God does the changing.

''Just finsihed the 60-day program and what a difference in my life after such a short period. It has freed me of all the petty fears and worries that have been plaguing me most of my life. I feel free and alive and ready to take on new challenges.

''I was glad to hear that others had trouble also. Sometimes, in time of personal problems, you tend to feel that you are all alone, and I definitely had some dark, dark days at the beginning. One message that I received that might be helpful to others was on the point of acceptance. I kept thinking that there were so many changes I needed to make in my life, and the more I tried to make those changes the more helpless and impotent I felt. Then I received the message that until I accept the moment exactly as it is presented, no changes can take place. But as I accept, I become one with the Power and God can then make any necessary changes in my life. The key is that God will make the changes, not me, the human. I do the accepting, God does the changing. I do the being, God does the doing.''

An inner peace that has nothing to do with the external situation.

''There have been so many marvelous things that have happened during these two months that even to briefly describe them would take a very long report. The most important impression that I had almost daily was the realization that much was taking place on a higher level of which I am not aware at this time. Much of it had to do with a 'new' friend from many past lives and the assurance that even though we were seldom together physically, we spent a lot of time on a higher spiritual level that greatly influenced our healing. Most of what took place on this higher level will be coming forth into our conscious awareness as we are open to it and as it is needed.

''Closely related to this was a feeling of peace in the midst of my daily activities...it made absolutely no difference whether the external situation was basically happy or most trying. It truly was an inner peace that has nothing to do with the external situation. I now know that I can have this peace at any time regardless of what the situation is—if I only accept it.

''Another impression was the assurance that through my long life I will always have everything I need to fulfill my purpose. The energy available for my use or misuse continues to grow. It is especially strong during meditation. More and more I am experiencing myself as a radiating center of power with awareness of my physical body diminishing. I am using this in some healing work that I am doing.

''Now that the program is over, it is time to begin: 'I have surrendered everything to Spirit'...''

Know that Spirit is doing and being everything now.

"I started on the non-human program on August 1. In my written agreement with Spirit I surrendered everything that came into my conscious mind...I surrendered my unemployed state AND my desire for a happy job situation. I surrendered the rental house in which we lived AND my desire to own a house, and much more. I immediately became aware of a happy spiritual release, and an abiding trust in Spirit grew in me as I consciously surrendered all problems and worries—knowing that 'Spirit is doing and being everything now.'

"On August 14 I was talking to a friend who was overtired and irritable with numerous unsolved problems. I had mentioned the 60-day program to her several times, and now offered again to assist her in getting started. She said angrily that she wasn't interested in 'that stuff' and didn't see where it had done me any good. I felt a twinge of pain but surrendered it to Spirit immediately and replied that I had been using the program for only two weeks. 'Regardless,' she said, 'you've been interested in that kind of stuff for a long time.' I went home and wrote in my diary: 'Dear Spirit, I'm counting on you, for I can do nothing of myself.'

"It is important for me to keep filling my mind with the message that marks out the path for me moment by moment, leading me to release every pain and every problem in the very moment of recognition—not giving it time to grow. This seems to be the key to maintaining the presence of Spirit. At first there is a lot of interference as one consciously strives to hold the presence, but after a while one is caught up in the flow as Spirit moves through your mind and life to take full command. The interruptions become fewer and farther between and hopefully, eventually are totally outgrown.

"On August 17 I started a new job, one that I had applied for but was totally indifferent about getting. In fact, I would have preferred any one of several others that I interviewed for, but it turned out to be a stepping stone to the job I was offered a month later in the same company—at a higher pay rate.

"At the end of October I moved into a home which I am buying. It's wonderful. And believe me, I couldn't have done this by myself. How did I get brave enough to apply for a loan, and who would grant a loan to someone who had been on the job for only a month? If I related all the details it wouldn't make it any easier to believe. All I know for sure is that I have surrendered all that I am and have to Spirit, and Spirit is doing and being everything.

"The non-human program has caused something to 'click' in my consciousness, some subtle understanding to seep through into my awareness that was previously blocked by factors beyond my understanding. I did not hear the 'click', but rather sensed a gradual inflow of contentment even in what previously seemed to be adverse circumstances. As I relaxed and let go of worrying, Spirit moved mountains for me with 'all deliberate speed.' I find that when I do all I know to do and surrender my efforts to Spirit, everything falls into place. I feel and visualize this happening within everyone throughout the world."

The challenges dissolve when the lessons are understood.

"The process of the 60-day program is so fascinating and revealing—sometimes excrutiatingly painful, and more often lately, blissful. I am learning to be nonresistant to and thankful for each so-called challenge because it is ripe with wisdom and understanding. Things, situations and feelings seem to be coming up so rapidly; I 'get it' and thank God. Or perhaps I should say that I thank God first and then 'get it.' Every situation, as soon as I surrender and thank the Spirit of Myself for it, absolutely is ripe with layer upon layer of understanding. I feel as if I am becoming lighter and lighter, and yet, paradoxically, more and more solid and grounded. I must add that the challenges seem to be dissolving as soon as the lesson is understood."

All things are possible when you are "open."

"After beginning the 60-day 'experiment' I received a call that I had been hoping for, for at least five years. But I didn't know then the reason I felt the need to talk to him. I know now that he is my soul mate (my first love of 30 years ago) and it has taken all these years for me to become 'open.'"

When we release our fears, the Law of Attraction works through a different vibration in consciousness.

"The experiment is flowing beautifully in my life. Since releasing all fears and worries (and more as they arise), I've attracted a beautiful, loving, fulfilling relationship to me with a man who shares my commitment to healing our planet as well as sharing life goals and a spiritual philosophy. We are teaching each other daily and are experiencing living fully in the moment in a way neither of us have done before. I have also tapped into an endless Source of Joy and inspiration for life. I am so filled up with love and joy that I just ask how I can serve Spirit's work every day. The timing is right on with the beginning of this brilliant experiment."

Simply remembering can reverse the situation and quiet the beast.

"I was delighted at the prospect as the experiment was laid out in the beginning. I began happily saying to myself, 'I can do that'! It wasn't long before every irritation and weak point in every condition and relationship was magnified to the MAX and I perceived myself failing time and again. In fact, I felt I had never behaved worse. Many times I was ashamed, disappointed and resentful that I couldn't do better.

"In the midst of the mess I discovered that remembering Myself and affirming that Truth, and then releasing to Spirit, the most feeble of glimmer of remembrance would begin to reverse the situation, smooth out the edges, and quiet the beast. I can't say that I have achieved total peace and harmony, but I learned that this so-called experiment is not an experiment at all. It is all there is and all there is to seek. At the risk of tempting my ego, I say again—'I can do that'!''

Learn to not judge yourself for the seeming weaknesses but to remember Who You are.

''It has been a very meaningful two months for me and I am not willing to end the experiment now. This is a lifetime commitment whether we know it or not. The first month was very easy for me to remember Who I AM for some reason. It was as if I had unseen help all of the time, and whenever a challenge came up it was easy to place it in the Spirit and release it. During the second month I was not so 'up' and seemed to forget for long periods of time, yet that was the month that so many issues were dealt with, so many prayers answered, so many worries solved. The best part of all, though, has been to learn not to judge myself for my weaknesses, but to remember that I AM SPIRIT. While I am remembering this, it is impossible to judge. The corollary to that is not to judge the judgements of others.''

As a non-human you will have the opportunity to test your wings.

''My whole concept of life, both spiritual and human, has made a 360 degree change. Now my Inner Self (Spirit) daily shepherds and leads my self (human ego) and it is so exciting and oh, so Divine. Deciding to continue daily and indefinitely the 60-day Spiritual Journey, I would like to share an experience that I had on Day 65.

''In the wee hours of the morning I experienced my first flying lesson. I actually left my earthly body for a time. My first recall is that suddenly my body was bursting with bright white light. The light left my body and there was in its place the Christ standing by my bed. Numerous angel forms glowed and hovered around the room. I was being helped and urged to leave my body and fly with them. I was afraid and my body seemed so heavy. I felt trapped—I wanted to fly but something seemed to be almost binding me to my bed. Christ and the angels were all the while almost literally pulling me upward and out to FREEDOM. Then it happened! I arose and flew up to the ceiling—and almost felt like a baby bird testing its wings, not smoothly but very jerky flying. Slowly, excitedly, I tried my wings. Then the thought hit me as I looked at my body on the bed—I must return to what I'm familiar with, element-wise. My body seemed like it was pulling me back like a magnet, and I was making both happy and moaning sounds at the same time. The room was so full of warm loving energy.''

Stop trying to do it yourself; let Spirit do the work.

''Embarking on the non-human program with great enthusiasm, I was at first filled with love, even a state of almost euphoria. Ah, but then later came the reaction as old buried resentments came rushing into consciousness, one after another and sometimes in bunches. It seemed that suddenly I didn't know how to love anyone. Old hurts presented themselves and it was all quite distressing. Then, just recently, I was able to 'give up' and the answer came: 'Stop trying to do this yourself. LET, LET, LET! Relax and LET God pour Pure Love THROUGH you! You can't do it yourself so let your High, Holy Self do the work'.

''This is what I am doing now, and believe me, it is wonderfully relaxing and fulfilling—and a lot more comfortable besides!''

You are given the opportuntiy to transmute the darkness once and for all.

''Like many others I experienced many challenges in all areas of my life and even had a better understanding of the phrase 'dark night of the soul.' It was also comforting when I found that I was not alone. It also confirmed what that little still voice kept telling me: 'Rejoice, you are being given the opportunity to transmute this once and for all.'

''Washing 'laundry' was not all that I did during the program. I received some new information and confirmation on previous information. The really interesting part was that the information was given to many different individuals at about the same time.''

Live for the joy of the moment.

''Just before midnight on January 31st, I finished the letter giving up my attachments to the Holy Spirit. I ended it by giving up the results of the experiment as well as the experiment itself. The next day I awoke with what seemed to be a sort of double vision where I was seeing the form and at the same time seeing the thought-life that was maintaining the form. This seeing included, but was not limited to, material objects. This all seemed very natural and it was some time before I realized that this was not my usual way of viewing things. With that awareness I remembered that I had entered into the 60-day experiment, and I thought, 'My God! If this is happening on day one, I wonder what day sixty will be like'.

''It was with that thought that the experience began to fade. By the next day it was only a memory. As I found myself trying to get the experience back I got depressed. The depression deepened. I'd work my way out only to tumble back again. The depression did not seem to affect my period of meditation. I then began to experience two intense desires: (1) I wanted to quit everything else and just sit, meditate, follow my breath, etc., and (2) I wanted to withdraw from the experiment and maybe leave the spiritual path entirely (I even thought that I might have already done so). At the same time I was aware that a part of me was mildly amused at all these goings on. Then I became unable to meditate—and then one day; ker-wham! I knew what had happened. I had tried to take the experiment back under my control. I had set up demands and expectations. I was living for the results of the future instead of for the joy of this moment. I had lost NOW, and that is indeed a loss. While the fleeting now-moment is not the Eternal Now, it does seem to be the gateway. It certainly has been an enlightening experience.''

There is only one condition.

Ralph Waldo Emerson gave us the secret of the non-human program when he said, ''this energy does not descend into individual life on any other condition than entire possession.'' Are you willing to give up everything in exchange for this sacred Light of Transformation? Are you ready to function on a higher plane of life? If your answer is an unqualified *yes*, the mystery of the Philosopher's Stone—that symbol of the perfected and regenerated individual—is waiting for you.

The title of this book is *A Spiritual Philosophy for the New World*. ''Spiritual'' means the ascendency of Spirit in individual consciousness and the reawakening to the Divine Identity, which is the effect or result of working only in the realm of Cause. ''Philosophy'' denotes the study of truth, the search for universal laws, and the love of wisdom—and represents the process and the system through which we find this Energy of Dominion.

Spiritual is the Truth, *Philosophy* is the Way, and *the New World* represents the Life of love, joy, peace and freedom that we will all enjoy as the collective consciousness shifts from darkness to Light. At some point on the scale, it will take only one more spiritually-infused person to tip the balance and cause a chain reaction of self-sustaining Good in this world.

You may be that person. The sequel to this book will be *your* story, your Book of Life. When completed it will be a record of your glorious journey—and you will see the mighty progress that you made in moving from the valley of shadows to the Mountain of Light.You came from a fearful, emotionally reactive human to that first level on the mountain where you made the commitment to seek the Way to the Top. As you donned the robe of the spiritual aspirant you were aware that "I of myself can do nothing," and with great humility you began to walk the sacred path. You were a beholder of the Spirit of God working through you to burn away the illusion, the sense of separation, and you joyfully cooperated by completely surrendering your life to Christ.

With discipline and dedication you ultimately detached yourself from the ego, your human sense of being, and you were suddenly lifted to another level of the mountain. Rising out of the depths of your consciousness now was the understanding that "I can do ALL THINGS through Christ"—through the strength, vision and power of the Great I AM. With the inner eye you saw the Truth of your Being and became of one accord with the Master Self, and you heard the words…"What do you want me to do for you? Command my hand." With great love the Master Teacher was offering you the wheel and the opportunity to drive your ship of life under the guidance of Divine Wisdom. The servant was learning mastery. With boldness and inspiration you began to work with the Divine Self to invoke only the Highest Good from the Highest Vision, and your world began to reflect the Light of Divine Reality. And you pronounced the works good, very good, and continued up the mountain.

In time came the Knowing. You had moved from "I of myself can do nothing"—to—"I can do All things through Christ"—to—"I AM ALL THINGS; I AM *THAT* I AM!" And in the twinkling of an eye the veil was shattered, all power in Heaven and Earth was yours, and you stepped forth into the world to serve. The servant had become the master in order for the master to become the servant…a World Server for God. And remember, "greater works" will you do.

It is time to begin.

It is time to finish the work.

APPENDIX

ANNUAL WORLD HEALING DAY

At noon Greenwich time, December 31, 1986, men, women and children around the world gathered to participate in the most comprehensive prayer activity in history—a planetary affirmation of peace, love, forgiveness and understanding involving millions of people in a simultaneous global mind-link. The purpose: to reverse the polarity of the negative force field in the race mind, achieve a critical mass of spiritual consciousness, and usher in a new era of Peace on Earth.

It was called World Healing Day, the World Instant of Cooperation, World Peace Day—a moment of Oneness to dissolve the sense of separation and return humankind to Godkind. Whatever the term or label, it was the New Beginning in restoring this world to sanity.

The majority of the individuals and organizations participating in this light of the World activity were operating under the umbrella of the Planetary Commission, a worldwide non-denominational, non-political organization without a headquarters, structure or staff. The Commission was and is simply a grass roots cooperative effort to unite people in a common bond of love and bring our planet back in balance.

The first formal announcement of the Commission was made on January 1, 1984, with the stated objective of having 500 million people on Earth consenting to a healing of the planet—with no less than 50 million meditating at the same time. December 31, 1986 was designated as "World Healing Day" and noon Greenwich was selected as the time for the healing meditation as it would encompass all time zones during that 24 hour period.

Word of this new Goodwill Task Force quickly spread, and when that "moment in time" arrived on December 31, 1986, the Mind-Link represented all religious faiths on seven continents, in more than seventy countries, and in every state in the U.S. Over 500 spiritual and peace-oriented organizations around the world participated.

Celebrations were held in cities throughout North and South America, Europe, Asia, Africa, India, and Australia. In the Soviet Union thousands gathered in Moscow to "think peace" and contemplate global cooperation.

In the U.S., a number of governors and mayors issued proclamations designating December 31st as World Peace Day, and gatherings involving thousands of people were held in areas and stadiums in major cities. Across America, other like-minded individuals came together in homes, churches, city parks, hotel ballrooms, in forests, and on mountains and beaches.

The Commission did not disband after December 31, 1986. In fact, it is expanding and gathering strength each year as greater awareness of the Event spreads around the world. Will you participate with us on December 31st of this year—and the next—and continue until the collective shift takes place? We ask that you join with other Light Bearers in your community, or if it is your preference, to be alone in coming into vibration with the Global Mind-Link to radiate your light, love and spiritual energy.

The World Healing Meditation that is being used by millions each year in the simultaneous bonding is shown on the following pages. Together we can usher in a New Beginning of Peace on Earth and Good Will toward all...as love flows forth from every heart, forgiveness reigns in every soul, and all hearts and mind are one in perfect understanding.

For more information on this Earth-changing Event, please write to the Planetary Commission for Global Healing, The Quartus Foundation, P. O. Box 1768, Boerne, Texas 78006-6768.

WORLD HEALING MEDITATION

In the beginning
In the beginning *God*.
In the beginning God created the heaven and the earth.
And God said Let there be light: and there was light.

Now is the time of the *new* beginning.
I am a co-creator with God, and it is a new Heaven
    that comes,
as the Good Will of God is expressed on Earth through me.
It is the Kingdom of Light, Love, Peace and Understanding.
And I am doing my part to reveal its Reality.

I begin with me.
I am a living Soul and the Spirit of God dwells in me, as me.
I and the Father are one, and all that the Father has is mine.
In Truth, I am the Christ of God.

What is true of me is true of everyone,
for God is all and all is God.
I see only the Spirit of God in every Soul.
And to every man, woman and child on Earth I say:
I love you, for you are me. You are my Holy Self.

I now open my heart,
and let the pure essence of Unconditional Love pour out.
I see it as a Golden Light radiating from the center of
    my being,
and I feel its Divine Vibration in and through me, above
    and below me.

I am one with the Light.
I am filled with the Light.
I am illumined by the Light.
I am the Light of the world.

With purpose of mind, I send forth the Light.
I let the radiance go before me to join the other Lights.
I know this is happening all over the world at this moment.
I see the merging Lights.
There is now one Light. We are the Light of the world.

The one Light of Love, Peace and Understanding is moving.
It flows across the face of the Earth,
touching and illuminating every soul in the shadow of
    the illusion.
And where there was darkness, there is now the Light
    of Reality.

And the Radiance grows, permeating, saturating every
    form of life.
There is only the vibration of one Perfect Life now.
All the kingdoms of the Earth respond,
and the Planet is alive with Light and Love.

There is total Oneness,
and in this Oneness we speak the Word.
Let the sense of separation be dissolved.
Let mankind be returned to Godkind.

Let peace come forth in every mind.
Let Love flow forth from every heart.
Let forgiveness reign in every soul.
Let understanding be the common bond.

And now from the Light of the world,
the One Presence and Power of the Universe responds.
The Activity of God is healing and harmonizing
    Planet Earth.
Omnipotence is made manifest.

I am seeing the salvation of the planet before my very eyes,
as all false beliefs and error patterns are dissolved.
The sense of separation is no more; the healing has
    taken place,
and the world is restored to sanity.

This is the beginning of Peace on Earth and Good Will
    toward all,
as Love flows forth from every heart,
forgiveness reigns in every soul,
and all hearts and minds are one in perfect undertanding.

It is done. And it is so.

ABOUT THE AUTHOR

John Randolph Price is co-founder with his wife, Jan, of The Quartus Foundation—the spiritual research and communications organization headquartered on The Guadalupe River Ranch in the Texas hill country north of San Antonio. They hold Spiritual Retreats and Intensive Gatherings at the Ranch several times a year, and conduct a Mystery School each February.

With Jan's assistance John has written more than ten books—and together they have appeared on radio and television in major cities across the nation discussing the new spiritual awakening taking place on Planet Earth, and have presented seminars and workshops on the theme of Self Mastery in more than a hundred New Thought churches. They have also been the keynote speakers at symposiums and conferences sponsored by the Association for Research and Enlightenment, the International New Thought Alliance, the United Church of Religious Science, and the Unity School of Christianity.

In 1984, they announced the Planetary Commission for World Healing, which called for a simultaneous global mind-link at noon Greenwich time, December 31, 1986—and continuing each year "until the last one comes into the Light." In recognition of this activity they were named the 1986 recipients of the "Light of God Expressing Award" by the Association of Unity Churches.

ABOUT THE QUARTUS FOUNDATION

The Quartus Foundation for Spiritual Research, Inc. is an organization dedicated to research and communications on the divinity of each individual. We seek to study the records of the past, investigate events and experiences of the present, and probe the possibilities and potential of the future through the illumined consciousness of awakened Souls.

Our objective is to continually document the truth that all men and women are spiritual beings possessing the powers of the cosmic realm—that each individual is indeed God individualized, and as this true Identity is realized, the person becomes a Master Mind with dominion over the material world.

The documentation comes through indepth research in Ancient Wisdom, Esoteric Philosophy, and New Thought Psychology—all of which reveal the healing, prospering, harmonizing Power of God working in and through individual being. We believe that the people on Earth are capable of rising above every problem and challenge that could possibly beset them, and that they are doing this daily in ways that are considered both "mysterious and miraculous." But in truth, the evil, the illness, the failure, the limitation, the danger, the injustice disappear through a change in individual consciousness.

What brought about the change? We seek to closely examine the problem and the solution, the activity of Mind and the Divine Laws, the cause and the effect—and to build a fund of knowledge based on the interrelationship of Spirit, Soul, Body and the world of form and experience.

We believe that what one person is doing to alter conditions and reveal order and harmony, all can do—and by researching and communicating specific examples of the Power at work, we can do our part in assisting in the general upliftment of consciousness. Through greater understanding, we can all develop a more dynamic faith in our Master Self, a conviction that

135

our potential is limited only by the scope of our vision, and a Knowledge that humankind is Godkind and does not have to accept anything less than Heaven on Earth.

For complete details on the activities of The Quartus Foundation and information on membership in The Quartus Society, write for a complimentary copy of The Quartus Report, P. O. Box 1768, Boerne, Texas 78006-6768.